Right to Life

The Pluralism of Human Existence

Parul Sharma

India Research Press

Right to Life : The Pluralism of Human Existence
Parul Sharma

India Research Press
Flat No.6, Khan Market, New Delhi - 110 003
Ph.: 24694610; Fax : 24618637
www.indiaresearchpress.com
contact@indiaresearchpress.com; bahrisons@vsnl.com

2007

ISBN thirteen: 978-81-8386-051-2
ISBN ten: 81-8386-051-6

Includes bibliographical references and index.
1. Human Rights – India / South Asia 2. Pluralism – South Asia .
3. Welfare – South Asia. 4. Women / Female – South Asia
I. Title. II. Author

Printed for *India Research Press* at Focus Impressions, New Delhi.

Contents

Dedicated to Biji,
thanks for everything…

Foreword

What are rights? Are rights mere semantic euphemisms or are they instruments that can be implemented and can be measured?

It is easier to say what is *not* a right. A right is not benevolence. It is not a mere gift or favour motivated by love, pity or a budget line. Rights are "... instruments that enable us to stand with dignity, if necessary to demand what is our due, without having to grovel, plead or beg or express gratitude when given our due, and to express indignation when what is our due is not forthcoming." A world with rights is a world in which people are dignified objects of respect, both in their own eyes and those of others. The validity of a right is absolute. Lack of normative application of the right does not affect the fact that it exists. Rights exist even when they are infringed.

What are the impacts of not having human rights in place? What changes for the child who is trafficked? What changes for the woman who is slapped by her husband? What changes for the student who is ragged and bullied as a fresher? What happens when you are labelled as a particular caste? What happens when you are denied an avenue to express yourself? What happens when an identity is forced on you?

What is impacted is the mental health of the person. The way she thinks, the way she feels. So, if human rights have to be the framework of any discourse, the language has to focus on the mental health of people. What is intended to be protected by human rights is not just the right to live, but the right to live with dignity. Dignity can be assured by using frameworks and skills of mental health.

The proposition of this book links rights to life and life to dignity; it recognizes the mental health of people at their operational point of vulnerability.

There are three ways of considering mental health from the perspective of rights. Firstly, wherein access to mental health services is seen as a right. Secondly, considering mental health impacts of situations where human rights are violated, such as violence against women, religion and caste based discrimination, sexual exploitation, neglect and abuse of children, etc. Thirdly, mental health being a prerequisite to achievements of the person's other rights. Mental health is a definitive universal need. It is a right. It needs to be recognized. The focus has to be on recognition of a broader concept of mental health beyond psychiatric disorders, by including mental health impacts of vulnerability and mental health as a fundamental in relation to implementation of other rights.

When mental health needs are not addressed, the human cost is large, for it is difficult to reclaim the person from the impact of his vulnerability. This book is a significant contribution in the journey reclaiming the person from the violation.

Achal Bhagat
MBBS MD MRC PSYCH (Oxford,UK)
Director of Saarthak, New Delhi, India

Preface

The idea of human rights has travelled a long way over centuries of ideological and philosophical discourses. Since 1948, the United Nations Human Rights framework has received wide acceptability. It recognizes the individual and his distinctiveness as the centre of social purpose. We enjoy human rights by virtue of being human. The Preamble of the Universal Declaration of Human Rights (UDHR) identifies the universality, indivisibility and interdependency of human rights accordingly:

" ...the ideal of free human beings enjoying freedom from fear and want can only be achieved if conditions are created whereby everyone may enjoy his economic, social and cultural rights, as well as his civil and political rights."

UDHR, together with two covenants, the International Covenant on Civil and Political Rights (ICCPR) and the International Covenant on Economic, Social and Cultural Rights (ICESCR) constitutes what is called the International Bill of Human Rights. The all-embracing right for any individual is to have the real option to live the life he himself values. To realize this, people must be free to exercise personal autonomy in planning their lives, from which it follows that they must enjoy all human rights. Civil and political rights on the one hand, and socio-economic rights on the other, independently of each other, are indispensable for the fulfilment of the all-embracing right. But, they also coexist and are interdependently reinforcing each other. If you do not have food and shelter, freedom of expression is probably a poor consolation. Neither is material security a satisfactory substitute for censorship.

A state cannot be called democratic without including these rights in its constitution and law framework and, as well, implementing them. Both these demands are imperative for a true democracy. India complies with the first requirement, which is manifested in the Preamble and in the statement on Fundamental Rights in the Constitution. The introductory words of the Preamble read:

"We, the people of India, having solemnly resolved to constitute India into a Sovereign, Socialist, Secular, Democratic Republic and to secure to all its citizens:
JUSTICE, social, economic and political;
LIBERTY of thought, expression, belief, faith and worship;
EQUALITY of status and opportunity;
And to promote among them all
FRATERNITY assuring the dignity of the individual and the unity and integrity of the Nation;
In our Constituent Assembly this twenty-sixth day of November, 1949, do hereby Adopt, Enact and Give to ourselves this Constitution."

With these words, India commits itself to sustain the values of social justice and welfare for its citizens. Yet, in India as in any other nation, there is a gap between a constitutional declaration and its implementation. Article 1 of the UDHR states: *"All human beings are born free and equal in dignity and rights. They are endowed with reason and conscience and should act towards one another in a spirit of brotherhood."* This statement is absolutely true, meaning that this is the way it ought to be. Yet, we know from observing real life, that this is not the reality, not in any nation. There are millions of people all over the world who are born into disadvantaged social circumstances. Article 1 is to be seen as a goal to be achieved. And, it is the obligation of the state to promote, realize and protect these rights. Citizens of a nation have a rightful claim on the state to accomplish this goal.

The gap between declaration and implementation in the Indian context is exposed in the particular challenge of the state's adherence to human rights and their enforcement when the rule of law is applied on disadvantaged groups such as the poor, women and children, Dalits (Scheduled Castes) or adivasis (Scheduled Tribes). In particular this concerns the Dalit community. In a society like India's, where caste plays a decisive role in defining people's societal positions, the concept of human rights takes on a specific meaning. In these cases, the unit of society is not the individual. The unit is caste and the rights that an individual has are not due to him personally. The right is due to him because he belongs to a particular caste. The Dalits, being at the bottom of the social hierarchy, are also today discriminated against in many spheres of society.

In her book *Right to Life: The Pluralism of Human Existence,* Parul Sharma assumes the holistic approach on human rights. She asserts that *right to livelihood* is an element of *right to life* under Article 21 of the Constitution. The Supreme Court has in a judgement from 1978 stated that the right to life provisions in the Constitution must be taken to mean the right to live with dignity. Throughout the book she elaborates on the contradiction between the guarantee of Right to Life in the Constitution and the understanding of what a functional life in dignity really means.

Parul Sharma affirms that criminal law and criminal procedural law are crucial fields for the defence of human welfare and esteem. Criminal cases, she says, are real reviews of a principle which is easily applicable to people living in a proclaimed welfare establishment where the individual can make appropriate and moralistically correct decisions. From this view she scrutinizes how the Indian state conforms to its commitments and how they are observed by law courts and in society as a whole.

With her book, Parul Sharma contributes to the understanding of the comprehensive meaning of human rights and of the important role of the judiciary in safeguarding human rights in its extensive meaning.

Hans Magnusson, Coordinator for India
Amnesty International, Swedish section.
Stockholm

Introduction

It gives me great pleasure to write this piece for this excellent book written by Parul Sharma. I have always been an admirer of Parul's writing, which not only displays her extensive research, deep insight and intensive thinking process but also utmost sincerity and commitment.

Ideally speaking, the right to life is an inherent right of every living being, which emanates from birth itself, but unfortunately this right has always remained dependent on the comparative strength of the creatures roaming on this planet. One may conclude that it is in accordance to the scheme of nature. However, I am not convinced, call me a sceptic if you like.

When this right is considered in the context of human beings, it takes varied dimensions. But one thing is certain, that this right is absolute. It is not dependent on the mercy of any system, society, government or constitution. Any action towards denial of this right is an infringement and a crime, may be by an individual or a group, even if it is backed by the sanction of a so-called 'Law'.

The right to life in the context of human beings goes with liberty and dignity. These are its essential dimensions, without which the right to life for a human being becomes meaningless. Liberty must be given a wider meaning which includes liberty to move freely, liberty to access information, liberty to express himself, liberty to pursue any profession (and develop skills for that) and liberty to build up capacity to enjoy liberty. Similarly, dignity means equal treatment, availability of food, clothing, shelter and other essentials for daily needs with mutual respect and without facing ignominy.

So, when we see that in this country about 80 per cent of the people are denied the essentials of their basic right, we are actually committing an infringement of this right and are thus guilty of a crime. I have no hesitation in saying that it is a man-made system, a generated situation, excuses of population explosion, etc. notwithstanding. The responsibility squarely lies with the class which controls the state machinery and which manipulates the so-called 'democratic elections' in such a way that the same class, maybe with changed masks, retains its control continuously. Poverty and deprivation, which are the result of inequalities and exploitation, are the weapons which cut at the root of the right to life.

Unfortunately, rather deliberately, the role of the state for this vast majority of people has always been restrictive. Moreover, it is also not enough to leave the field open for all and declare it as an 'opportunity providing set up'. This virtually facilitates the rich and the powerful class to grab all the opportunities for itself and continue exploitation. The role of the state should actually be restrictive for these classes and enabling for the vast poor and deprived majority, helping them to build up their capacity to actually comprehend and enjoy the right to life in its true sense.

As already said, the right to life is absolute. However, it can at the most be restricted in case someone becomes harmful either for an individual or society as a whole (and not only the ruling class). But in any case, this right cannot be taken away altogether. This holds good even for extreme cases. This is a matter of conviction and truth, and as they say, convictions and truth can only be tested in extreme situations. There are no ifs and buts and no exception is to be carved out. A reader will find a very elaborate analysis and forceful arguments on this angle in this book.

Even otherwise, in the present decayed judicial system, only those are liable to be condemned who do not possess the means either to win over or browbeat the system. Thus, capital punishment also remains reserved for the poor and weak. Nobody can vouch for the infallibility of the judiciary which is already completely insensitive and highly oriented against the poor and the deprived. Stray cases here and there by the higher judiciary also remain empty verbosity and do not percolate in actual practice. One example will be enough. Anti-beggary laws actually criminalize poverty. They do not solve any problem. On the contrary, they dehumanize the helpless. These laws must be struck down at first glance not only as being ultra-vires of the Constitution but also for being anti-humanity and the very antithesis of the right to life. But the apex Court, in its insensitive wisdom, has done quite otherwise. It has asked the authorities to strictly implement these laws.

I hope this book will be widely well-received. The thought-provoking material will prove to be an important milestone in the struggle for human rights.

Premkrishna Sharma
Advocate, Labour Law and Human Rights
Supreme Court of India
President Rajasthan People's Union for Civil Liberties
(PUCL) 1998 - 2004).
Vice-President, Delhi PUCL
Jaipur, India

The Concept

This book is an effort to interlink social conditions in society with the guarantee of the Right to Life as enshrined in the Indian Constitution. The paradigm shift of economic and social rights, from being valued as a need to becoming full-fledged legally binding rights, must be viewed in the larger social context while legislating laws and pronouncing laws. A rights-based approach is founded on the conviction that each and every human being, by vir-tue of being human, is a holder of rights. A right entails an obligation on the part of the government to respect, promote, protect and fulfil it. The strong legal and normative character of rights and the associated governmental obligations are based on international human rights treaties and other standards, as well as on national constitutional human rights provisions.

Olga Tellis vs Bombay Municipal Corporation came before the Supreme Court as a writ petition from slum dwellers and the homeless in the city of Bombay. They prayed against the order of eviction and that they be allowed to continue to stay on the pavements. The respondents, the State of Maharashtra and Bombay Municipal Corporation, had decided to forcibly evict all pavement and slum or *busti* dwellers in Bombay, based on Section 314 of the Bombay Municipal Corporation Act, 1888. The order of the Bombay Municipal Corporation for eviction was challenged as being unreasonable and unjust and without providing an alternative living facility. The petitioners claimed the right to livelihood as part of their right under Article 21 of the Constitution, which is the right to life.[1] Many authors and writers have claimed that the Supreme Court in *Olga Tellis*, in its decision took an activist approach, based on humanitarian elements. Such a view indicates that humanitarian elements are conventionally excluded from judicial decisions. The Supreme Court held that the slum dwellers must get alternative shelter if they are evicted from the pavements. The eviction orders were held to be invalid under Article 14 and 19 of the Constitution. In fact, the right to life was once again enlarged to include the right to livelihood as being a part of the liberty of an individual. The decision of the Court also focused on the concept of the welfare state and reliance, though not expressly but impliedly, was placed on the Directive Principles of State Policies under the Constitution. The judgement underlined:

"An equally important facet of that right is the right to livelihood because, no person can live without the means of living, that is,

---

1. Compare, *Ram Prasad vs Chairman, Bombay Port Trust* (AIR 89, SC 1306) (in which the Indian Supreme Court directed the relevant public authorities not to evict 50 slum dweller families unless alternative sites were provided for them). *Francis Coralie vs Union Territory of Delhi* (AIR 1981, SC 746) (in which, building upon Maneka Gandhi, the Indian Supreme Court stated that the right to life includes the right to live with human dignity and all that goes along with it, namely the bare necessities of life such as adequate nutrition, clothing, and shelter). *Maneka Gandhi vs Union of India* (1978, 1SCC 248) (a seminal case in which the Indian Supreme Court stated that the right to life provisions in the Constitution must be taken to mean the right to live with dignity').

the means of livelihood. If the right to livelihood is not treated as a part of the constitutional right to life, the easiest way of depriving a person of his right to life would be to deprive him of his means of livelihood to the point of abrogation."

The Court stated in paragraph 46 of the judgement: "*Human compassion (happiness) must soften the rough edges of justice in all situations."* Elaborating this statement with regard to the right to life and human rights, it is here that the psychological notion of *empathy* must enter law making and legal pronouncements. This book will deal further with this idea while discussing the social chain. The effects that deprivation of basic economic and social entitlements has on the dignity of a person must not be ignored in the Court of Law, whether the person is a beggar or a child. There is a constant contradiction between the guarantee of Right to Life and the understanding of what a functional life really is with legislation and judgements. In order to understand human rights the law maker has to understand human life, whether this is the human life of a group of individuals such as beggars, or individuals such as child victims. This book will focus on such clashes and contradictions within the issues of Capital Punishment, Child Rights, Women's Rights and the Right to Mental Health. In *Excel Wear vs Union of India*, one of the judges underlined that the word "life" in Article 21 of the Constitution does not mean mere animal existence.[2] Furthermore, the right visualised by this article is to live a

2. AIR 1979 SC 25.

dignified life. In the context of State Responsibility, it is important to understand that the right pronounced in Article 21 must be understood as one of the duties of the Welfare State.

This book is an effort to analyse how the notion of a dignified life is actually understood in its limited form by the law and legislator in India. A dignified life must include those elements which have been viewed as narrow features or insignificant areas of life, aspects such as, for instance, the right to be informed about sexual conduct and sexual misconduct, the right to receive mental health support the moment a traumatic incidence occurs, the right to be equal before a court of law without taking into consideration matter you are a woman, man or a child, and the right to have your special needs taken into consideration. Right to life must include an understanding of all the different kinds of social contexts prevailing in India. An understanding of the Right to Life must include a strong social awareness of why and how situations occur. If such aspects continue to be denied by the law and the legislator, the right to life may not go beyond mere animal existence.

Currently, one issue receiving attention in India is to prescribe capital punishment for rapists. The former Deputy Prime Minister, L.K. Advani, has on several occasions proposed the death penalty for rapists. It is incredible how politicians constantly talk of the death penalty for sexual offenders, and completely overlook the right to mental health of the victim/survivor. The minister further stated that the Indian government held the view that rape should attract the most deterrent penalty.[3]

A crucial part of the sentencing process must include an overall victim's perspective, where the law- maker constantly scrutinize and balance the offender's rights with those of the victim. All aspects concerning victimology must be understood as a direct link to the question of Right to Life and Livelihood of the victim of the crime. Arguments of deterrence and severe punishments are viewed in a legal and social context, as the sole consolation for a victim.

Research and professional experience shows that secondary victimization, generated either by institutions or individuals, is often experienced by victims in the aftermath of a crime and leaves them in need of help. Secondary victimisation involves a lack of understanding of the suffering of victims which can leave them feeling both isolated and insecure, losing faith in the help available from their communities and professional agencies. The experience of secondary victimization intensifies the immediate consequences of crime by prolonging or aggravating the victim's trauma. Unsympathethic attitudes, behaviour, and acts of commission or omission can leave victims feeling alienated from society as a whole.

Secondary victimization in itself is not an unusual

3. See *The Times of India* , October 28, 1998, "Capital punishment for rapists soon", says Advani.

phenomenon in our society. It most recently appeared in an Indian courtroom on May 3, 2005, when a convicted rapist proposed marriage to his victim. The man was convicted of raping and seriously injuring a 22-year-old nurse in September 2003 at the hospital where they both worked. Minutes before sentencing was due on May 3, he issued his marriage proposal. Postponing the sentence until the next day, the judge asked the victim whether she would accept the proposal from her attacker, who had hoped it might soften his sentence. The victim told the court she had rejected the offer.

Did the court as a carrier of justice at all consider the danger to women caused by such a precedent? If the convicted rapist said he was offering to marry the woman because the stigma of rape in India meant that no one else would, do both the judiciary and the law also have the same pattern of thinking? What social responsibility was the court fulfilling? In the cases of assault against women, statistics from 2000 show that a woman is raped every hour in India. Still, victims are often reluctant to report the rape. In court, they are supposed to prove that the rapist sexually penetrated them in order to get a conviction. This can be damaging, mainly so when defence counsel use harsh and callous rhetoric to further victimize the survivor. Eminent judges and landmark cases talk of rape not being merely a physical assault, but that it is often destructive of the whole personality of the victim. "...a rapist degrades the very soul of the helpless female". Furthermore, it has also been realized that courts should shoulder a great responsibility while trying an accused on charges of rape. It has been felt that such cases must be dealt with "utmost sensitivity". Unfortunately, and following old patterns, the court has not defined what is meant by great responsibility or sensitivity. Could it be that the court is referring to rehabilitation and/or mental health support for the victim?

Remarkable developments have taken place both internationally and nationally when it comes to prioritizing child rights, but the links between child abuse, child labour and the care for a child's mental health are still absent. In India, there is no separate law with regard to sexual assault of children. The general law on rape contained in the Indian Penal Code covers child sexual abuse and assault. Similarly, the Juvenile Justice Act, 1986 and the amended Act of 2000, have impressive preambles, but despite this, the Act scarcely touches upon the subject of child sexual abuse, and completely ignores therapy and mental health considerations.

Several aspects within Women's Rights and Child Rights' issues highlight the insensitivity and disinterest amongst law and policy-makers when it comes to real victimology, and the psychological understanding of a victim's trauma. With regard to the victim and the application of psychological considerations and support, the criticism indicates how the application of the capital punishment is viewed to be the settler of justice for victims. However, applying this punishment and completely disregarding rehabilitation and social assistance, as recommended in the Declaration of Basic Principles of Justice for Victims of Crime and Abuse of Power, adopted by the United Nations through General Assembly resolution 40/34 of November 29, 1985, cannot be a matter of a justice system balancing the rights of the victims with the rights of the offenders. In *Sakshi vs Union of India*, the Supreme Court of India asked the Law Commission to consider certain important issues regarding sexual abuse of children submitted by the petitioner and the feasibility of amendment to Sections 375 and 376 IPC.[4] Hopefully, the forthcoming amendment will also deal with aftermath issues of child sexual abuse. Abused children usually suffer from serious mental and physical after-effects, either immediately or later in life, from emotional and behavioural problems to abnormal sexual behaviour and psychiatric disorders. Suicidal tendencies and drug abuse are common long-term effects as well. Child-related concepts are gravely missing in Indian laws. So, where do we bring our affected children for justice, when the law looks away from crimes relating to them?

A victim of a crime, and more so if the victim is a child, who is undergoing trauma, needs to be treated with care. The facilities with regard to emergency reception of victims of crime is lacking to a great extent. There are no mental health professionals to deal with trauma-stricken victims. Moreover, the victims, who do not show signs of serious physical injury, are released immediately without any

4. (1999) 8 SCC 591.

psychiatric treatment. There are also no provisions in the Mental Health Act to admit a person suffering from psychiatric illness for treatment in emergency.

In the case of *Majlis Manch vs State of Maharashtra & Ors.* a nine-year-old deaf and mute girl institutionalized in an observation home was raped. The medical examination indicated "Skin injury mark. Bite mark on right cheek and multiple abrasion marks over skin, buttocks and both legs". Even after such a dreadful case, where the child was not able to express pain or explain even minimally what had happened to her, there has been no realization or will to make mental health considerations an inextricable component of law. [5]

The legal notion of right to life becomes insincere if an inclusive viewpoint, with regard to human life, is not taken. Right to life becomes an incomplete notion if necessities of life, emotional and physical, are ignored. Such necessities may be the right to sex education and the right to mental health. *Right to Life : The Pluralism of Human Existence* is much too often compromised within the Indian context, whether it is the right of an offender or a victim, the notion is just not understood or linked to human needs.

For a dignified life, in the name of justice,

Parul Sharma , Stockholm, Sweden.

---

5. Criminal Writ Petition No.585 of 2000-Bombay High Court.

1. The Welfare State and Human Life

A Welfare Analysis – as a part of the judicial process. Criminal law and criminal procedural law are crucial fields for the defence of human welfare and esteem. Criminal cases are real reviews of a principle which is easily applicable to people living in a proclaimed welfare establishment, where the individual can make appropriate and morally correct decisions. The same parameter applies to socially unadjusted people, the mentally insane, and reformable and unreformable criminals. The Directive Principles of State Policy, contained in Part IV of the Indian Constitution, the guiding principles to be followed in the governance of every state, embody the concept of a Welfare State. The Supreme Court of India has, in several judgements, held that the principles supplement the fundamental rights in achieving a Welfare State. Clearly, the aforesaid is a core, which is about achieving a welfare existence by and through judicial review.

The Indian Constitution: The Directive Principles of State Policy and Social Objectives
The Fundamentals of the Indian Legal System

The Indian Constitution. India inherited a complex legal system. The legal system today both looks and sounds as if it was Common Law. The British, in particular, would like to claim it is. It is certainly based on the Common

Law system, but has an entirely different application and outlook today.[6] The first draft of the Constitution of India was prepared in October 1947 by the Advisory Branch of the Office of the Constituent Assembly. The Assembly, on November 26, 1949 adopted the Constitution of India.

Significances in the Constitution. The Constitution is the lengthiest-ever given to any nation. It has a very comprehensive nature, and contains fundamental rights as well as duties. The fundamental duties are guidelines for the State and its people. The Constitution is the fundamental and supreme law of the land and creates the Legislature under which all the laws of India are to be enacted.

Interpretation of the Constitution. The Supreme Court of India has stated that unless otherwise indicated, every word in the Constitution is supposed to have been used in its normal or ordinary connotation and should be given the

---

6. *Common Law* is a system based on the Doctrine of *Stare Decisis*, that is the principle of case law entirely based on the methods applied in England set by historical factors. Common Law is that part of English law based on rules developed by the royal courts during the first three centuries after the Norman Conquest (1066). In the Continental system, the judge's duty is basically to interpret the statutes by using different norms of interpretation. But in the system of Common Law the judge is considered to be a lawmaker. He forms the law according to the situation which has occurred. In the case of India, one could say, that it is a mix of the two, since it has a codified Constitution, but many provisions are meant to be literally interpreted by judges still having a strong desire to maintain the Doctrine of *Stare Decisis*.

plain common sense meaning.[7] It is thus understood that the Constitution has to be interpreted in the liberal manner and not in a narrow sense, according to *the Doctrine of Liberal Interpretation*.[8]

Former Chief Justice of India A.S. Anand in a lecture indicated that the judiciary has "to act as a balancing mechanism between the conflicting pulls and pressures operating in a society... to develop and adapt the law so as to meet the challenges of contemporary problems of the society and respond."[9] These legal facts are very important to remember for the issue of the capital punishment and Article 21 of the Constitution.

The Indian Penal Code (IPC) The Indian Penal Code was enacted in the spirit of British rule in India. The framers of the Indian Penal Code provided for capital punishment, but with the remark that the same should be applied selectively. The idea of having such a Penal Code was inherited from the British legal mentality at that time. The British introduced Common Law and transplanted it in India, hence, some scholars claim that the Indian system is a pure transplant of the British legal system.

The Code of Criminal Procedure (Cr.P.C.) Capital punishment was enacted as the rule by the Cr. P.C. 1898, for a number

---

7. *Keshavananda Bharati vs State of Kerala* (1973) 4 SCC 225).
8. Kashyap, Subhash C., *Our Constitution, An Introduction to India's Constitution and Constitutional Law*, p.5, second edition, (1995).
9. Verma, Sharad, *Our Legal System in Crisis*, The Lawyers Collective, August 1998,Volume 27.

of offences. However, it is claimed that India was influenced by moves to abolish the penalty.[10] Some minor changes took place as a result. For instance, before the amendment of the Cr. P.C. in 1955, it was mandatory for the court to give reasons for not awarding the death sentence in a case of murder. However, post-amendment, it was no longer necessary. Under the new Cr. P.C. in 1973 the court has to give reasons for sentencing a persn to death and it narrows the use of capital punishment.

The 1973 Code has some procedural safeguards. In Section 354 (3) of the Cr. P.C. (the so-called death reference cases):

I. Effective opportunity to the accused to represent against award of death sentence (according to the Supreme Court of India this means that the accused has a chance for a separate hearing after the conviction, on a separate day).

II. The sentence is not final till it is considered and confirmed by the High Court, irrespective of whether the accused appeals.

III. A right to appeal to the Supreme Court wherever sentence of the trial court is varied by the High Court and capital punishment is imposed.[11]

---

10. Mahajan, V.D., *Jurisprudence and Legal Theory*, p. 151, fifth edition, (1987).
11. Bhatt, S. Ravindra, *A Question of Life, Reflections on Capital Punishment*, The Lawyers Collective, July 1998, Volume 4. Also see Ratanlal and Dhirajlal, *The Code of Criminal Procedure*, 15th edition (1997).

The punishments to which offenders are liable under the provisions of the Indian Penal Code are firstly, death; secondly, imprisonment for life; thirdly, imprisonment which is of two descriptions, namely (i) rigorous, that is, with hard labour (ii) simply; fourthly, forfeiture of property; and fifthly, a fine.

Section 302 of the Indian Penal Code already possesses an inbuilt method of substantial punishment. Two penalties are there—life imprisonment is the rule, and death sentence is an exception. According to the Supreme Court, capital punishment is an extraordinary sentence. Capital punishment is applicable only in situations of murder. There is no alternative punishment whatsoever apart from these two.

The Directive Principles of State Policy. Part III of the Indian Constitution guarantees "fundamental rights" to all citizens. Some of these, like the right to life (Article 21), and the right to equality (Article 14), apply to all persons. The fundamental rights are enforceable in the High Courts and the Supreme Court. In writ petitions before these courts, a person or a citizen can seek enforcement of fundamental rights and redress for their breach. Judicial review of executive action as well as of legislation and judicial and quasi-judicial orders is recognized as part of the Basic Structure of the Constitution, which cannot be taken away even by an amendment to the Constitution.[12]

---

12. *Keshavananda Bharati vs State of Kerala* (1973), 4 SCC 225 (cited hereafter as the Fundamental Rights case).

The Supreme Court has the final word on the interpretation of the Constitution, and its orders, being law, are binding and enforceable by all authorities—executive, legislative and judicial.[13]

The Directive Principles of State Policy (DPSP) are contained in Part IV (Articles 36 to 50) of the Indian Constitution. Many of the provisions correspond to the provisions of the International Covenant of Economic, Social and Cultural Rights (ICESCR). For instance, Article 43 provides that the state shall endeavour to secure, by suitable legislation or economic organization or in any other way, to all workers, agricultural, industrial or otherwise, work, a living wage, conditions of work ensuring a decent standard of life, and full enjoyment of leisure and social and cultural opportunities. In particular, the state shall endeavour to promote cottage industries on an individual or cooperative basis in rural areas. This corresponds more or less to Articles 11 and 15 of the ICESCR. However, some of the ICESCR rights, for instance, the right to health (Article 12)have been interpreted by the Indian Supreme Court to form part of the right to life under Article 21 of the Constitution, thus making it directly enforceable and justiciable.[14]As a party

---

13. *Union of India vs Raghubir Singh* (1989) 2 SCC 754 at 766 para. 7. Article 142 of the Constitution declares that any order of the Supreme Court is enforceable throughout the territory of India and Article 144 mandates that all civil and judicial authorities shall act in aid of the Supreme Court.
14. *Francis Coralie Mullin vs The Administrator, Union Territory of Delhi* (1981) 2 SCR 516.

to the ICESCR, the Indian Parliament has enacted laws giving effect to some of its treaty obligations and these laws are, in turn, enforceable in and by the courts. Article 37 of the Constitution declares that the DPSP "shall not be enforceable by any court, but the principles therein laid down are nevertheless fundamental in the governance of the country and it shall be the duty of the state to apply these principles in making laws." It is not a mere coincidence that the apparent distinction that is drawn by scholars between the ICCPR rights and ESC rights holds good for the distinction that is drawn in the Indian context between fundamental rights and DPSP.[15] Thus the bar to justiciability of the DPSP is spelled out in a sense in the Constitution itself.

When the struggle for primacy between fundamental rights and DPSP came up initially before the Supreme Court, the court stated: "The directive principles have to conform to and run subsidiary to the chapter on fundamental rights."[16] Later, in the Fundamental Rights Case, the majority opinion reflected the view that what is fundamental in the governance of the country cannot be less significant than what is significant in the life of the individual. Another judge constituting the majority in that

---

15. D. J. Ravindran, *Human Rights Praxis: A Resource Book for Study, Action and Reflection* (Bangkok: Asian Forum for Human Rights and Development, 1998), p.124, where he questions the validity of the view that civil and political rights are human rights and economic, social and cultural rights are only aspirations.
16. *State of Madras vs Champakam Dorairajan* (1951) SCR 525.

case said: "In building up a just social order it is sometimes imperative that the fundamental rights should be subordinated to directive principles."[17] This view, that the fundamental rights and DPSP are complementary, "neither part being superior to the other," has been the definition since.[18]

The DPSP have, through important constitutional amendments, become the benchmark to insulate legislation enacted to achieve social objectives, as enumerated in some of the DPSP, from invalidation by courts. This way, legislation for achieving agrarian reforms, and specifically for achieving the objectives of Articles 39(b) and (c) of the Constitution, has been immunized from challenge as to its violation of the right to equality (Article 14), and freedoms of speech, expression, etc. (Article 19). However, the court has retained its power of judicial review to examine if, in fact, the legislation is intended to achieve the objective of Articles 39(b) and (c); and where the legislation is an amendment to the Constitution, whether it violates the Basic Structure.[19] Likewise, courts have used DPSP to uphold the constitutional validity of statutes that apparently impose restrictions on the fundamental rights under Article 19 (freedoms of speech, expression, association, residence,

---

17. Mathew, J. in the Fundamental Rights case, note 1 above, SCC para. 1707, p. 879.
18. V. R. Krishna Iyer, J. in *State of Kerala vs N. M. Thomas* (1976) 2 SCC 310 at para. 134, p. 367.
19. *Minerva Mills vs Union of India* (1980) 3 SCC 625; *Waman Rao vs Union of India* (1981) 2 SCC 362.

travel and to carry on a business, trade or profession), as long as they are stated to achieve the objective of the DPSP.[20]

Most importantly, the DPSP are seen as aids to interpret the Constitution, and more specifically to provide the basis, scope and extent of the content of a fundamental right.

It is important to note that fundamental rights have themselves no fixed content; most of them are empty vessels into which each generation must pour its content in the light of its experience. Restrictions, abridgement, curtailment and even abrogation of these rights in circumstances not visualized by the Constitution Fathers might become necessary. Their claim to supremacy or priority is liable to be overturned at particular stages in the history of the nation by the moral claims embodied in Part IV.

Under the Constitution, the obligations of the State are clearly demarcated, but, unfortunately, they are not prescribed in clear terms. While the fundamental rights of the individual can be enforced by direct access to the Supreme Court, the Directive Principles of State Policy, which deal mainly with socio-economic rights of the community at large, *are not enforceable through any approach to courts*. Article 37 specifically provides that "this part shall not be enforceable by any court but the principles therein

20. For instance, Article 43, dealing with living wages and conditions of work, has been relied upon to sustain the reasonableness of the restriction imposed by the Minimum Wages Act, 1948. *Chandra Bhavan vs State of Mysore* (1970) 2 SCR 600.

laid down are nevertheless fundamental in the governance of the country and it shall be the duty of the state to apply these principles in making laws."

It is most important to note that Article 37 does not, directly or indirectly, prohibit the court to analysis in order to detect whether these socio-economic rights are purposeful or not. As long as there is no sanction attached to a detection it cannot fall within the definition of enforceable as stated in Article 37. The Court's mandate to analyse as to why a crime occurred, and due to which economic and social failures, cannot fall within the notion of enforceable.

It is necessary to consider at this juncture the meaning of the word "socialism" envisaged in the Preamble of the Constitution. Establishment of an egalitarian social order through rule of law is the Basic Structure of the Constitution. The Fundamental Rights and the Directive Principles are the means, like the two wheels of a chariot, to achieve the object of democratic socialism. The word "socialist" used in the Preamble must be read from the goals Articles 14, 15, 16, 17, 21, 23, 38, 39, 46 and all other cognate articles seek to establish, i.e. to reduce inequalities in income and status and to provide equality of opportunity and facilities. Social justice enjoins the Court to uphold the government's endeavour to remove economic inequalities, to provide a decent standard of living to the poor, and to protect the interests of the weaker sections of society so as to assimilate all sections of society in a secular integrated socialist Bharat with dignity of person and equality of status to all.[21]

21. AIR 1997 SC 3297.

Viewed in this context, in cases where capital punishment is a potential ruling, a welfare analysis, however difficult it may seem, has to be conducted by the court in order to detect whether elements of a functional or non-functional Welfare State may have had an effect on the case—without justifying the crime. Components of this analysis should be understood as a livelihood test, based on the definition of livelihood stated in case law, under Article 21 of the Constitution, namely, *that no one can live without the means of living, that is, the right to livelihood.*[22] People most endangered are not necessarily the people living on the borderlines of society those who are materially unadjusted, but also those who are emotionally unadjusted. In practice, this would suggest a deeper sociological aspect to case analysis both at the level of the court of law and the casework prepared by lawyers. The welfare analysis should ideally be a momentum with the Court, where the same applies to an inquisitorial procedure.[23] This system of criminal justice

22. (1995) 3 SCC 42: 1995 SCC (L&S) 604 and LIC of India vs Consumer Education and Research Centre (1995) 5 SCC 482. Right to economic equality is held to be a fundamental right in *Datmia Cement (Bharat) Ltd. vs Union of India* (1996) *10 SCC 104 : JT*(1996) *4 SC 555*. Right to shelter was held to be a fundamental human right in *P.G. Gupta vs State of Gujarat*, 1995 Supp (2) SCC 182 : 1995 SCC (L&S) 782 : (1995) 30 ATC 47, *Shantistar Builders vs Narayan Khimalal Totame* (1990) 1 SCC 520, *Chameli Singh vs State of UP* (1996) 2 SCC 549 and *Ahmedabad Municipal Corporation vs Nawab Khan Gulab Khan* (1997) 11 SCC 121 : JT (1996) 10 SC 485.
23. This methodology is inspired by the system of criminal justice, namely the inquisitorial procedure, in force in some European countries, but not in England, in which the truth is revealed by an inquiry into the facts conducted by the judge. It is the judge who takes the initiative in conducting the case, rather than the prosecution or defence; his role is to lead the investigations, examine the evidence, and interrogate the witness.

would enable the court to trace the social chain, to analyse whether justice has been a birthright in the case of both the victim and the accused. Here, it is suggested that the judicial process functions as an instrument to trace social injustice, and to trace the crime and not the criminal. The aforesaid guarantees *stare decisis*, the maxim expressing the underlying basis of the doctrine of precedent.

The Common Law method and its adaptability to new circumstances guarantees a welfare order. The bridge between a systematic welfare analysis and the law is most crucial in less developed countries such as India.[24] Here, it is not a matter of expanding the law, but an inclusion of a constitutional expression. The real protection of the notion of welfare lies in the adjudication of the courts and the curtailing of executive discretionary power. This safeguard is summed up in the Rule of Law, but this effect can hardly be established by constitutional proclamations, it is the

24. Starvation deaths. Shatar (Jharkhand). At least 14 people have died of starvation in Jharkhand's Shatar area. Poor monsoons and government apathy have been blamed for these deaths. Carved out of Bihar, Jharkhand is rich in minerals and forests but its vast resources lie largely untapped or are pawned to rich landowners who rarely share profits with the impoverished masses. The state received 27 per cent less rainfall this season, prompting the central and state government authorities to release Rs. 8.8 crores as interim drought relief. Villagers, however, said that not a penny had reached them. Shrey Kewat, whose ageing and severely malnourished mother died because of hunger, is now struggling to keep his wife and two children alive. "She (Kewat's mother) died due to hunger. She did not get food, was sick and could not get treatment. When there is nothing to eat, how can we get medicines? She died because she had no strength left because of the lack of food." Source: *The Hindu, September 21,* 2004.

product of a long process resulting in a degree of freedom for the courts from political interference.

Welfare Analysis: The Code of Justice

"To establish an egalitarian social order, the trinity, the Preamble, the Fundamental Rights in Part III and Directive Principles of State Policy in Chapter IV of the Constitution delineated the socio-economic justice. The word 'justice' envisioned in the Preamble is used in a broad spectrum to harmonize individual rights with the general welfare of the society. The Constitution is the supreme law. The purpose of law is realization of justice whose content and scope vary depending upon the prevailing social environment. Every social and economic change causes change in the law. In a democracy governed by rule of law, it is not possible to change the legal basis of socio-economic life of the community without bringing about any corresponding change in the law. In interpretation of the Constitution and the law, an endeavour needs to be made to harmonize the individual interest with the paramount interest of the community keeping pace with the realities of ever-changing social and economic life of the community envisaged in the Constitution. Justice in the Preamble implies equality consistent with the competing demands between distributive justice with those of cumulative justice. Justice aims to promote the general well-being of the community as well as the individual's excellence. The principal end of society is to protect the enjoyment of the rights of the individuals subject to social order, well-being and morality."[25]

---

25. (1996) 10 SCC 104.

Justice is mostly described as a moral ideal that the law seeks to uphold in the protection of right and punishment of wrongs.[26] Justice is not restricted to time or a point of time, before or after a crime is committed. It is a process and starts from the point of birth. Justice Suba Rao, the former Chief Justice of India, rightly remarked: "Social justice must begin with child. Unless a tender plant is properly nourished, it has little chance of growing into a strong and useful tree. So, the first priority in the scale of social justice should be given to the welfare of children."[27] In contrast, it is worthwhile underlining that the little-understood legal notion of social justice is not included nor defined in any recognized dictionary of law. Analysing the aforesaid, clearly, what I would like to call, a social chain has to be considered. It is from the point of birth that the notion of justice or social justice becomes attached to an individual, the child. This is an inherent birthright, which attaches the *responsibility of protection of welfare* on the State. It is a *judicial guarantee* given by the State to the individual. It is of utmost importance for the lawyer, the legislator and the court to understand the link between social justice and justice. For long, justice has been confined to the law, with regard to crime, punishment, and the settling of disputes before courts. The claim that it is irrelevant to expressing unfair distribution of resources in society can never achieve and lead to balanced judicial pronouncements. It is worth mentioning the UK Commission on Social Justice and their summarization of social justice into four principles, namely:

---

26. *The Oxford Dictionary of Law*, Oxford University Press.
27. Suba Rao, *Social Justice and Law* (1974), p. 110.

1. The foundation of a free society is the equal worth of all citizens.

2. Everyone is entitled, as a right of citizenship, to be able to meet their basic needs.

3. The right to self-respect and personal autonomy demands the widest possible spread of opportunities.

4. Not all inequalities are unjust, but unjust inequalities should be reduced and where possible eliminated.[28]

A welfare analysis would seek to trace the welfare components in a case—a scrutiny of society's structure, resulting in a thorough review of the status of economic and social rights in a state.[29] This analysis would, furthermore, remove bias in judgements, which may appear due to the judge's background and personal history. Here again, it must be underlined that the methodology proposed does not seek to justify crime. Nor does it seek to prove interlinks between crime and poverty. Given the economic and social order in developing states, a welfare analysis would enhance the micro and macro aspects of the delivery of justice to the people. The methodology should be regarded as a protector of socio-economic rights and justice. This may

28. Jane Franklin (edited), *Social Policy and Social Justice*, Cambridge (England), Polity Press (1998), p. 48.
29. *International Covenant on Economic, Social and Cultural Rights*, Adopted and opened for signature, ratification and accession by General Assembly, resolution 2200A (XXI) of December 16, 1966, *entry into force,* January 3, 1976, in accordance with Article 27.

not be as crucial a methodology in Western democracies as it is in states where social justice is far from obtained.

In T.H. Marshall's classic article, *Citizenship and Social Class*, social rights are contrasted with political and civil rights. Political rights guarantee opportunities to participate in the political process. Civil rights define areas of non-interference, which create opportunities for private action. Social rights refer to a wide spectrum of claims:

From the right to a modicum of economic welfare and security to the right to share to the full in the social heritage and to live the life of a civilized being according to the standards prevailing in the society.[30]

X born	**X commits crime**	**X punished**
Social Justice **State Responsibility**	→	**Justice** **State Responsibility**

The above diagram suggests that unless social justice is recognized as a basis for pure justice, the court will not be able to produce pronouncements based on justice. The presumption should be that the two sides of justice are actually two sides of a single process, where society and the individual belong to a process of rights resulting in just pronouncements. However, what must not be presumed by the court is that social justice is guaranteed in society. Hence, the need for a welfare analysis. Scholars over time

30. T.H. Marshall, *Citizenship and the Social Class*, p. 74.

have pointed out that social justice should not only be seen as a mechanism granting the satisfaction of needs alone, but that it also includes protecting the status of people as full members of the community. The law should have no contradiction, if the aim, which is justice-based social justice is taken care of. One crucial point which emerges is the maximization of a Welfare State through actualization, where the analysis is translated into recommendations formulated to enhance the welfare concept.

Social justice is the comprehensive means to remove social imbalances by law harmonizing rival claims or interests of different groups and/or sections in the social structure or of individuals by means of which alone it would be possible to build a Welfare State. The ideal of economic justice is to make equality of status meaningful and life worth living, at its best, removing inequality of opportunity and of status — social, economic and political.[31]

Dr. B.R. Ambedkar, in his closing speech in the Constituent Assembly on November 25, 1949, had elucidated thus:

"... What does social democracy mean? It means a way of life, which recognizes liberty, equality and fraternity as the principles of life. These principles of liberty, equality and fraternity are not to be treated as separate items in a trinity. They form a union of trinity in the sense that to divorce one from the other is to defeat the very purpose of democracy. Liberty cannot be divorced from equality,

31. (1996) 10 SCC 104.

equality cannot be divorced from liberty. Nor can liberty and equality be divorced from fraternity. Without equality, liberty would produce the supremacy of the few over the many. Equality without liberty would kill individual initiative. Without fraternity, liberty and equality could not become a natural course of things. It would require a constable to enforce them. We must begin by acknowledging the fact that there is complete absence of two things in Indian society. One of these is equality. On the social plane, we have in India a society based on the principle of graded inequality, which means elevation for some and degradation for others. On the economic plane, we have a society in which there are some who have immense wealth as against many who live in abject poverty. On January 26, 1950, we are going to enter into a life of contradictions. In politics we will have equality and in social and economic life we will have inequality. In politics we will be recognizing the principle of one-man one vote and one vote one value. In our social and economic life, we shall, by reason of our social and economic structure, continue to deny the principle of one-man one value. How long shall we continue to live this life of contradictions? How long shall we continue to deny equality in our social and economic life? If we continue to deny it for long, we will do so only by putting our political democracy in peril. We must remove this contradiction at the earliest possible moment or else those who suffer from inequality will blow up the structure of political democracy which this Assembly has so laboriously built up." [32]

---

32. B. Shiva Rao (ed.), *The Framing of India's Constitution: Select Documents, Vol. IV*, pp. 944-45.

2. Capital Punishment and the Right to Life in India

The Social Contract

> Sentencing is part of a very complex system. Many events and agencies influence the decision, and sentencing can cause anything from a ripple to a tidal wave throughout the system. And so sentencing, in common with other stages in the criminal justicc process, cannot be viewed in isolation.[33]

The Constitution of India is not merely a legal document. It is also a social document providing for a social contract, whose goals are achieved through the fundamental rights and directive principles. Social contract is a phrase used in political science and sociology to denote a real or hypothetical agreement within a state regarding the rights and responsibilities of the state and its citizens, or more generally, a similar concord between a group and its members. All members within a society are assumed to have agreed to the terms of the social contract by their choice to stay within the society. The social contract, as a political theory, explains the origin and purpose of the state, and of human rights. The essence of the theory, in its most common form, namely the one proposed by Jean-Jacques Rousseau, is as follows: In order to live in society, human beings agree to an implicit social contract, which gives them certain rights, such as the right to life, in return for giving

33. P. Morgan, D. Moxon and R. Tarling, *The Implications of Sentencing for the Criminal Justice System* (1987), p.169.

up certain freedoms they would have in a state of nature, such as the freedom to kill others.[34] Thus, the rights, and responsibilities, of individuals are the terms of the social contract, and the state is the entity created for the purpose of enforcing that contract. Also, the people may change the terms of the contract if they so desire; rights and responsibilities are not fixed or "natural". However, more rights, according to Rousseau, always entail more responsibilities, and fewer responsibilities always entail fewer rights.[35]

After comprehending the meaning of social contract, it becomes essential to define precisely Article 21 from a social point of view:

Article 21 Protection of Life and Personal Liberty
No person shall be deprived of his life or personal liberty except according to procedure established by law.

Undoubtedly, the right to life has been recognized by the

34. Rousseau's ideas were influential at the time of the French Revolution although since popular sovereignty was exercised through representatives rather than directly, it cannot be said that the Revolution was in any sense an implementation of Rousseau's ideas. The primary principles of Rousseau's political philosophy is that politics and morality should not be separated. When a state fails to act in a moral fashion, it ceases to function in the proper manner and ceases to exert genuine authority over the individual. The second important principle is freedom, for preserving which the state is created.
35. *The Social Contract,* 1762.

jurisprudence of the nation and its Constitution as the most precious right of them all, a right without enjoyment of which no other right is possible. Seemingly, the right to life is not only the basis for applying the law, but a fundamental instrument to achieve the correct application of law. A "right to life reasoning", must be understood as the application and the aspiration in law. In the context of a social contract, protection of life must logically be understood as a process and not only the starting point in judicial reasoning. This process fails whenever there is scope for limiting the right to life.

India, however, retains capital punishment through Article 21 of the Constitution, which allows the State to deprive any person of the right to life provided that it is done by a procedure established by law. Section 53 of the Indian Penal Code (IPC) also lists 'death' as one of the forms of punishment that may be imposed for an offence. However, such power is not arbitrary, and it must conform to prescribed substantive and procedural safeguards, pass the test of reasonableness, and be subject to judicial review. Furthermore, this position is not static and has been constantly subject to change by legislative amendment and judicial interpretation.

In the original Criminal Procedure Code (CrPC) of 1898, Section.367 (5] provided death as the usual punishment for capital offences, requiring judges to provide justification in writing if they passed a sentence of life imprisonment instead. Capital punishment was believed to be the normal punishment, and only under extenuating circumstances could life imprisonment be awarded as in *Rishideo Pandey vs State of UP.*[36] In 1955, however, the 26th Amending Act removed this provision and the extent of punishment was left to the discretion of the court. There was a further shift away from neutrality when, in 1973, the Supreme Court upheld the constitutionality of the death penalty but established that capital punishment should be a narrow exception and not the rule in *Jagmohan Singh vs State of UP.*[37]

In 1977, the Supreme Court further developed the principle establishing life imprisonment as the rule, and capital punishment as the exception, in *Asgar vs State of UP.*[38] In *Bachan Singh vs State of Punjab*, capital punishment was challenged on the grounds that:

1. It was irreversible and could, given the fallibility of the process of legal mechanisms, result in the execution of innocent people;

2. No convincing evidence existed to prove that capital punishment served a legitimate penological interest and

3. Execution regardless of the means chosen or the offence involved constituted a cruel inhuman and degrading punishment.[39]

---

36. AIR 1954 SC 706.
37. (1973) 1 SCC 20.
38. AIR 1977 SC 2000.
39. AIR 1980 SC 898.

The Court, by a majority of 4 to 1, including the then Chief Justice, while rejecting these arguments, set out important limitations on awarding the sentence of death. In its most significant departure from earlier jurisprudence on the subject it stated: A real and abiding concern for the dignity of human life postulates resistance to taking life through law's instrumentality. That ought not to be done save in the rarest of rare cases, when the alternative option is unquestionably foreclosed.

In *Macchi Singh vs State of Punjab*, the court summarized the propositions set out in *Bachan Singh* and explained the task of a sentencing judge:

> A balance sheet of aggravating and mitigating circumstances has to be drawn up and in doing so the mitigating circumstances have to be accorded full weight and a just balance has to be struck between the aggravating and mitigating circumstances before the option (to award the death penalty) is exercised.[40]

The Rarest of Rare Cases

The Supreme Court has listed various factors to be considered in determining whether a case should be considered one of the rarest of rare.

1. Manner of commission of murder – whether death of victim caused by torture or other cruelty

40. AIR 1983 SC 957.

2. Motive for murder – whether crime involved total depravity and meanness

3. Anti-social or socially abhorrent nature of the crime – murder of a member of Schedule Caste or minority community arousing social wrath or involving 'bride burning' or 'dowry death'

4. Magnitude of the crime – multiple murders of members of a family or particular caste, community or locality and

5. Personality of the victim of murder – an innocent child, helpless, old or infirm or a public figure murdered for political rather then personal reasons.

The Rule of Law

Justice Bhagwati, in his authoritative dissent in Bachan Singh's case, had held that it is an essential element of the rule of law that the sentence imposed must be proportionate to the offence. Capital punishment cannot be regarded as proportionate to the offence of murder, merely because the murder is brutal, heinous or shocking. The nature and magnitude of the offence or the motive and purpose underlying its commission cannot have any relevance to the proportionality of capital punishment to the offence. Therefore, it was argued that capital punishment is arbitrary and unreasonable. Below is a dramatic revelation of the unscientific application of law, and it becomes essential to define the legal notion of the Rule of Law, which is the supremacy of law.[41]

Perhaps the most famous exposition of the concept of Rule of Law was laid down by Albert Venn Dicey in his *Law of the Constitution* in 1895 :

> When we say that the supremacy or the rule of law is a characteristic of the English constitution, we generally include under one expression at least three distinct though kindred conceptions. We mean, in the first place, that no man is punishable or can be made to suffer in body or goods except for a distinct breach of law established in the ordinary legal manner before the ordinary courts of the land. ...
>
> ... every official, from the Prime Minister down to a constable or a collector of taxes, is under the same responsibility for every act done without legal justification as any other citizen. The Reports abound with cases in which officials have been brought before the courts, and made, in their personal capacity, liable to punishment, or to the payment of damages, for acts done in their official character but in excess of their lawful

41. *The Oxford Dictionary of Law*, fourth edition, Oxford University Press.

> authority. [Appointed government officials and politicians, alike] ... and all subordinates, though carrying out the commands of their official superiors, are as responsible for any act which the law does not authorize as is any private and unofficial person. [42]

The definition of the Rule of Law will inevitably lead to guarantees for the same to survive and be sustained. Most importantly, such interpretations have to be made in the context of the right to life and its application universally as well as nationally. An important component such as the Rule of Law must be incorporated in the interpretation of right to life. However, this understanding is, in practice, non-existent, as can be seen from the above. One ruling justification for declaring Rule of Law a practical instrument for national lawyers in their regular practice is to assert it and Constitutional Law as interdependent instruments which are naturally equal. From an even more scientific perspective, it must be understood that the Rule of Law and jurisprudence become, if they are not merged, incomplete and dysfunctional. The element of social development should be the core in judgments, understanding, and interpreting jurisprudence in a more target-oriented manner. On a national level, until Rule of Law and Constitutional Law become at par with each other, the right to life will become merely an instrument

42. *Law of the Constitution*, London, Macmillan, 9th ed. (1950), p.194.

of activism outside the courtroom—most of the time provoking legal systems. In the case of capital punishment, it is at the cost of lives that judges are neglecting the concept of the Rule of Law.

Justice Bhagwati's underlining the Rule of Law makes it necessary to scrutinize the notion. One critical reason for the abolition of the death penalty is the fault of arbitrariness in sentencing judges. It is the judges who choose between death and lesser punishment, and this choice has remained subjective and discriminatory. The apex court has said that capital punishment ought not to be imposed except in the "rarest of rare cases". Pronouncing these four words has become a routine, more than application of science, before the judge pronounces death. By masking the notion of rule of law, the arbitrary choice of the sentencing judge has led us into a complacent belief that the sentencing judge has made the right choice between life and death.

It becomes a must to ask how one may distinguish between an ordinary murder and a "rare" murder, and among "rare" murders, how does one find the double purified essence of "the rarest" murder? Well, it obviously helps to describe a murder as brutal, heinous, as judges invariably do. An ordinary person could fairly so characterize every murder. Ultimately, judges award the capital punishment or life depending on their own sensitivity and value system. Each judge will easily find "special reasons" for awarding the death sentence according to his own perception of the gravity of the murder.

Even in the *Bachan Singh* case, Justice Bhagwati mentioned the problem of this delicate matter by stating: "What may appear to be special reasons to one judge may not so appear to another." Justice Bhagwati, unfortunately, did not elaborate further. What is important to note is the variation in understanding and recognizing jurisprudence and the effects of the same on a particular case.

A Constitution Bench of the Supreme Court, however, refused to raise this custom to the "pedestal of a rule" as it argued that doing so would essentially mean leaving the sentence to the determination of one judge, in *Babu and 3 Others vs State of UP.*[43] It is indeed unfortunate that the Court overlooked the larger requirement of unanimity in favour of the concern that one judge could hold the others at ransom. Thereby the Court overlooked the importance of removing all doubts and safeguarding the fairness of the judicial system. The Indian Supreme Court had another opportunity to rectify its position, when the case of *V. Mohini Giri vs Union of India,* was argued before it in 2002.[44] In this case the petitioner had sought "the issuance of a guideline as to what should be the appropriate approach in the cases where one of the judges in the Bench of this Court while hearing an appeal against death sentence, acquits the accused person". The Apex Court declined to issue such a guideline, arguing that it would curtail the judicial discretion of the bench.

---

43. AIR 1965 SC 1467.
44. 2002 AIR SCW 5306.

The position of Indian courts with regard to awarding non-unanimous death sentences is of particular concern because of the number of cases where death sentences and executions carried out have been found to be erroneous. The Liebman Report in 2000, concluding a 23-year study conducted by Columbia University, of the US, found that 68 per cent of all death sentences awarded were reversed due to serious legal error.

The non-compliance with the Rule of Law essence was so clearly demonstrated in a case in the Indian Supreme Court in 1981. Jeeta Singh, Kashmira Singh and Harbans Singh had all played an equal part in the ghastly murder of a family. Because separate petitions were made to the Supreme Court by each of the convicts, one bench of judges of the Supreme Court rejected the first petition of Jeeta Singh who was later executed. A different bench of judges, which commuted his sentence to life imprisonment, heard Kashmira Singh's petition. On the eve of his execution, Harbans Singh's petition came before yet another bench of Supreme Court judges, who when coming to know of Kashmira Singh's case, directed that the case should be sent back to the President for reconsideration of his clemency petition.

> Justice Bhagwati stated: "This is a classic case which illustrates the judicial vagaries in the imposition of death penalty." Former Chief Justice Y.V. Chandracud noted: "The course which this case has taken makes sad reading. Three persons were sentenced to

> death by a common judgement and, regretfully, each one has eventually met with a different fate."

While the Devender Pal Singh Bhullar case is well-documented for the large number of procedural lapses by the police, it also highlights the issue of non-unanimity leading to a failure of the Rule of Law.[45] Devender Pal Singh Bhullar was one of five members of the Sikh separatist organization Khalistan Liberation Force (KLF), accused in 1993 of involvement in a plot to assassinate the Indian Youth Congress President. Bhullar was sentenced to death by a Designated Court for offences under the Terrorist and Disruptive Activities (Prevention) Act, on the basis of an uncorroborated confession, while the other co-accused were acquitted for lack of evidence against them. Bhullar maintained that this 'confession' was neither voluntary nor true, but fabricated, and that his signatures had been forcibly obtained on partly written and blank papers.

The dissenting judge, M.B. Shah, in the appeal before the Supreme Court, noted his suspicion of the investigating authorities and the 'confession'. The other two judges, who upheld the trial court's death sentence, stating that a voluntary confession required no corroborative evidence and was enough to convict the accused, did not endorse this view. Referring to the requirement of proof beyond reasonable doubt as "merely a guideline and not a fetish", the majority judgement observed, "Exaggerated devotion

45. (2002) 6 SCC 81.

to the rule of the benefit of the doubt must not nurture fanciful doubts or lingering suspicions and thereby destroy social defence. Justice cannot be made sterile on the plea that it is better to let a hundred guilty escape than punish an innocent". The judgement further noted, "the non-observance [of procedure] does not cause any prejudice to the accused..." Procedure is the handmaid and not the mistress of law, intended to subserve and facilitate the cause of justice. The majority judgement set down some potentially damaging and incongruous propositions of law, contrary to established principles of the criminal justice. It restricted the scope and application of the presumption of innocence, the requirement of non-arbitrary procedure and reduced the standard of evidence required to prove the facts beyond reasonable doubt.

In contrast, the dissenting judge, who acquitted the accused of all charges, noted the lack of substantial evidence and discrepancies in procedure, pointed to the involuntary nature of the statement of the accused, and highlighted the unfairness of the sentence due to the acquittal of the other four accused. The use of the majority rule, however, meant that capital punishment was confirmed.

A review petition was filed, firstly contending an apparent error on the face of record and, secondly questioning the validity of the imposition of the death penalty taking into account that the senior-most judge of the Supreme Court bench had expressed dissent.[46] Justice Shah's minority

46. AIR 2003 SC 886.

judgement, in this instance, laid down a proper premise for the Bench to review the order of capital punishment if one of the three judges gives a different, and lesser sentence — e.g. preferring life imprisonment to capital punishment.

The minority judgement suggested that, "such an approach is consistent with Article 21 of the Constitution as it helps saving a human life from the gallows and at the same time putting the guilty accused behind the bars for life". He argued for a sound precedent to be laid down, whereby the dissent of one judge "... be regarded sufficient to treat the case as not falling within the narrowed ambit of 'rarest of the rare cases when the alternative option is questionably foreclosed'". Once again however, the majority judgement upheld the capital punishment.

The Bhullar case remains one of many where capital punishment has been awarded despite dissenting opinions on either guilt or punishment. Where judges disagree on the guilt of the accused, the dissent may be sufficient to constitute reasonable doubt. Furthermore, dissent on punishment also raises serious concerns about the applicability of the 'rarest of the rare' principle.

The Supreme Court in "Humanist Moods"

In Mohammed Chaman's case, the accused had raped and killed a girl, aged one and a half. The Supreme Court, while describing the crime as "undoubtedly heinous and reprehensible" took a "humanist approach" and changed the capital punishment to life imprisonment. Four days, after the execution of Dhananjoy Chatterjee, who was sentenced to death for raping and murdering a 14-year-old girl in Kolkata in 1990, the Supreme Court commuted the capital punishment on one Rahul who had raped a four-year-old girl and then slit her throat. The same day a session's judge in Ahmedabad sentenced one Kishan Marvadi to death for the killing and rape of a schoolgirl of six years, describing the murder as "heinous and devilish".

Hanging by Neck: "Quick and Certain"

It is important to note the case of *Inderjeet vs State of Uttar Pradesh*, where it was concluded that a punishment which is too cruel or torturesome is unconstitutional.[47] This case does not comply with all the various aspects of capital punishment. For instance, the question which was examined in *Deena vs Union of India* was whether hanging by neck to execute a capital punishment can be said to be violative of Article 21, on the ground that it is a cruel method of taking life.[48] This submission was not accepted. After examining all other methods prevalent in the world of taking lives, it was felt that hanging was in operation in large parts of the civilized world and consists of a mechanism which is easy to assemble and is free from anything that would unnecessarily sharpen the poignancy

47. AIR 1979 SC 1867.
48. AIR 1983 SC 1155.

of the prisoner's apprehension and is quick and certain, eliminating, at the same time, the possibility of a lingering death, because of unconsciousness, which supervenes almost instantaneously after the process is set in motion and death follows as a result of the dislocation of the cervical vertebrae. It was further pointed out that the system of hanging as now used avoids to the full extent that chances of strangulation, which results on account of too short a drop or of decapitation which results on account of too long a drop. It was observed that this process of execution was being conducted with decency and decorum without involving degradation or brutality of any kind.

It is with regard to the above that public hanging was regarded as barbaric and violative of Article 21, in *Attorney General of India vs Lachma Devi*, by which the order of the Rajasthan High Court to carry out capital punishment by public hanging at the stadium ground of Jaipur after giving the case widespread publicity in the media about the date, time and place of prosecution.[49] The Bench opined that public hanging was a revolting spectacle "harking back to earlier centuries". It was further observed, "a barbaric crime does not have to be visited with a barbaric penalty, such as public hanging". Hence, concluding from the aforesaid case, when a hanging is public it becomes barbaric, when it is not public it is a civilized operation of justice.

49. AIR 1986 SC 467.

The Royal Commission on Capital Punishment 1949-1953 in India, found that hanging is the most 'humane method of execution'. The Commission, involving lawyers and psychologists, came to the conclusion that the dislocation of the neck hardly gives any pain nor does it take time.

Justice Bhagwati, in the Bachan Singh case has carefully discussed this particular execution. In short, references were made to American data by taking the statement of a warden of a prison in the US, describing in general how the prisoner goes through the very distressing experience of being weighed and measured the day before execution, etc. This is to assure breaking of the neck. There are times, the warden said, when the neck has not been broken and the prisoner strangles to death. His eyes almost pop out of his head, his tongue swells and protrudes. In 1927, again in the US, a surgeon witnessed a double execution and stated that of the supposed corpses, one made respiratory efforts after being cut down from the rope after hanging there for fifteen minutes.

There is no doubt also that hanging involves immense physical pain and suffering. Strangely, the usage of foreign material, both in the Royal Commission Report and in Justice Bhagwati's reasoning in the Bachan Singh case, is used as the main source of examination. Whereas, materials and data from the jails of India and statements from Indian wardens would serve the purpose even more, and make it easier for an Indian judge to relate to it. This statement by the American warden is regularly used by

NGOs against capital punishment.[50] This fact shows that there certainly is a lack of internal statements from personnel in Indian jails.

The 35th Law Commission Report: India's Social Specialities

The Law Commission of India had gone into the issue of capital punishment, in its 35th report. This report consists of a careful study into each detail of importance using all proper resources available. The report is naive in almost all aspects. It involves District, Sessions and High Court Judges, advocates from all levels (senior as well as juniors), the Bar Association, etc. In the report, comparative studies of Europe, the US and Sri Lanka were conducted. The very conclusion of the report was the favouring of the retention of the penalty, largely based on the likelihood of its deterring grave capital crimes such as murder. The gravity of murder is explained as the "crime of crimes".[51] The belief is that such an application of the penalty in question really decreases the incidence of murder in the long run is the common link that runs through the whole report.

The report also stressed the circumstances and conditions in India. As a matter of fact, the method used in the report is based on a concentration on the social structure in India, the so-called extra-legal factors. This was done in the report by drawing parallels to the social specialities in India—by

50. For instance, the statement has been used by People's Union for Democratic Rights, New Delhi, in their pamphlet against *Judicial Terror.*
51. See paragraphs 131-135 in the Law Commission Report.

declaring the absence of education, prosperity, homogeneity, and viability in many parts of India.

Many lawyers in India still actively use these arguments on the social structure. The statement in the 35th Law Commission report was that the arguments used against and for the penalty could have different outcomes depending on what society we are dealing with. The conclusion was that the poor people of India actually needed something that was deterrent – capital punishment. What was not thought to be deterring in other countries was deterring enough in India. The outcome of this report was the enactment of the 1973 Code of Criminal Procedure.

Delay in Execution

Another crucial aspect of the violation of Article 21 is the delay in the carrying out of the death sentence. Whether delay in capital punishment affects Article 21 has been the subject matter of a number of decisions of the apex court. The view taken in *T. V. Vatheeswaran vs State of Tamil Nadu* was that delay constitutes exceeding two years in the execution of the punishment. The offender would be entitled to invoke Article 21 in such cases.[52] Furthermore, in such delays the quashing of capital punishment could also be demanded and the punishment commuted to life imprisonment. A different view, however, was taken in *Sher Singh vs State of Punjab*, where the former decision was

52. AIR 1983 SC 361 (2).

overruled by stating that the delay exceeding two years would not be enough by itself to demand quashing of the capital punishment and to get it commuted. "The fixation of time limit of two years does not seem...to accord with the common experience of the time consumed by the litigative process and the proceedings before the executive".[53] In *Javed Ahmed vs State of Maharashtra*, it was felt that it was not quite appropriate for the Sher Singh Bench to overrule the decision. It was further stated that to meet the call of Article 21, the procedure, no matter at what stage, must be fair, just and reasonable and that a prisoner cannot be tortured or subjected to unfair or inhuman treatment. What was overruled in Sher Singh's case again became a principle.

Article 21 stands like a sentinel over human misery, degradation and oppression. Its voice is the voice of justice and fair play. That voice can never be silenced on the ground that the time to heed its imperatives is long since past in the story of trial. It reverberates through all stages—the trial, the sentence, the incarceration, and finally, the execution of the sentence.[54]

Mental Torture and Article 21

The two-year rule was again overruled in *Triveni Ben vs State of Gujarat*.[55] This question subsequently came up in

---

53. AIR 1983 SC 465.
54. AIR 1985 SC 231.
55. AIR 1989 SC 1335.

Madhu Mehta vs Union of India. Here, the Bench opined that a speedy trial, which is a part of the fundamental right to life and liberty, is no less important for disposal of a mercy petition and observed that it has been universally recognized that a condemned person has to suffer a degree of mental torture even though there is no physical mistreatment and no "primitive" torture.

The observations of Justice Shetty in Triveni Ben were quoted to the effect:

> As between funeral fire and mental worry, it is the latter which is more devastating, for, funeral fire burns only the dead body, while the mental worry burns the living one.[56]

Having noted that the mercy petition had remained pending for eight years, the Bench opined that there were no reasons sufficiently commensurate to justify such a long delay, and because of the mental agony suffered of living under the shadow of death for long, far too long, it held that the prisoner should not suffer that agony any longer and altered the punishment to life imprisonment.

"Be hanged by the neck until dead": A History of Hanging

The term capital comes from the Latin *capitalis*, meaning head. Therefore, capital punishment is the penalty for a

56. AIR 1989 SC 2299.

crime so severe that it deserves decapitation. Hanging is one form of capital punishment. Hanging may involve breaking of the neck through drop-hanging, which can cause instant unconsciousness without breathing, and quick death, or one or more of the following:

- closing the airway
- closing the carotid arteries
- closing the jugular veins
- carotid reflex (which reduces heartbeat when the pressure in the carotid arteries is high) causing cardiac arrest

Hanging has been used as a punishment throughout history. The classic sentence involving hanging is that the condemned person "be hanged by the neck until dead". A more elaborate sentence, once used for particularly atrocious crimes, for instance high treason in England, was for the person to be "hanged, drawn and quartered". Because of its association with crime and criminals, many consider hanging a method of execution that causes shame to the victim, since historically, it is associated with 'common' criminals. The feudal England peasants were usually hanged for crimes, but the nobility were beheaded. [57]

Hence, courts in the post-World War II war crimes trials in Germany and Japan pronounced hanging for war criminals rather than execution by a firing squad. As a form of judicial execution in England, hanging is thought to

57. See, Elisabeth Tuttle Orman, *The Crusade against Capital Punishment in Great Britain*, London, Stevens (1961).

date from the Saxon period, *circa* 400 AD, although earlier the Persian Empire had used it too. Records of the names of British hangmen begin with Thomas de Warblynton in the 1360s; complete records extend from the 1500s to the last hangmen, Robert Leslie Stewart and Harry Allen, who conducted the last British executions in 1964.

Early methods of hanging merely involved a hangman's noose on a rope placed around the victim's neck, with the loose end thrown over or tied to a tree branch; the hangman then drew up the criminal, who gradually strangled. An early refinement had the victim climb a ladder or stand in a cart that the hangman then removed. The 1800s saw the development of a machine that used weights to draw the victim aloft. A further development had the victim step onto a metal plate, triggering the weights so that it was the victim that effectively started the process. As the number of executions increased, purpose-built gallows, which usually consisted of two posts joined by a crossbeam, replaced trees. Soon virtually every major town and city in Britain had its own gallows.[58]

Until 1808 the law in Britain offered capital punishment for some 200 offences, including attempting suicide, being in the company of gypsies for one month, vagrancy for soldiers and sailors, and "strong evidence of malice" in children aged 7-14 years old. A variety of loopholes in

58. See, George Ryley Scott, *The History of Capital Punishment: Including and Examination of the Case for and against the Death Penalty*, London : Torchestream Books (1950).

British criminal law, together with judicial leniency, tempered the law's tendency to prescribe hanging for what many would today consider minor offences. First-time offenders could escape a capital punishment for some crimes through the benefit of clergy, and of those criminals actually sentenced to death, many were later pardoned. Only about half the capital punishments pronounced at common law in the 18th century were carried out, and by the beginning of the 19th century, growing doubt over the appropriateness of capital punishment led to nearly 90 per cent of British capital sentences being commuted to lesser punishments.

Between 1832 and 1834 Parliament abolished capital punishment for:

1. shoplifting goods worth five shillings (£0.25) or less,
2. returning from Transportation,
3. letter-stealing, and
4. sacrilege.

In 1861 the British Parliament reduced the number of capital crimes to the following:

1. murder,
2. treason,
3. arson in Royal Dockyards, and
4. piracy with violence.

Britain abolished public hangings in 1868, and formally abolished the hanging, beheading, and quartering of traitors in 1870. Although hangmen had introduced the "drop" by the late 1700s, it was initially only a substitute for the ladder or the cart. The first popular practitioner of "the drop" was William Calcraft. However, his successor, William Marwood, who was often quoted as saying "Calcraft *hanged* them, I *execute* them", introduced the "long drop". Marwood realized that each person required a different drop, based on the prisoner's weight, which would dislocate the cervical vertebrae resulting in "instantaneous" death. A process of gruesome experimentation led to the discovery that energy of 1260 foot pounds (1710 joules) would have the desired effect, so one could calculate the required drop by dividing 1260 by the weight of the victim: a person weighing 112 pounds (50.8 kg) required a drop of 11.25 ft (3.43 m). Later, Marwood refined this basic formula to take account of the prisoner's age, stature, and physical condition, especially after some early mistakes when too great a drop resulted in decapitation. Marwood also experimented with the positioning of the knot, and discovered that placing it under the left ear or under the angle of the left jaw would jerk the head backwards at the end of the drop and instantly sever the spinal cord and dislocate the cervical vertebrae. Little by little, hanging became more of a science than an art. By the mid-20th century the average time between taking a victim from the cell and death was around fifteen seconds, although on May 8, 1951 Albert Pierrepoint conducted the fastest hanging on record when James Inglis, whom a court had only three weeks earlier convicted and sentenced for the murder of a prostitute, was pronounced dead only seven seconds after leaving his cell.

3. Poverty and Formal Punishment

Of utmost importance to the Indian context is one report which concludes:

> ...the threat of legal sanctions is reduced by constraints of poverty, drug use, criminal peers, lack of normative constraints...[59]

Stephen Baron's interests relate to the study of criminology. His work is primarily in the area of street youth and their criminal behaviour as well as public attitudes towards juvenile justice. He is conducting a research project that examines how situational factors in disputes influence the use of violence by street youth and is beginning a project that examines how poverty and unemployment influence street youth's involvement in crime and substance abuse. The study explores the effects of the threat of formal punishment on the criminal behaviour of homeless male street youth, paying particular attention to how these threats are shaped by their living conditions and other factors in their lifestyles. Results reveal that while many street youth fear legal sanctions, more serious offenders do not. Instead, their poverty, drug use, association with criminal peers, and missing normative constraints reduce their fear of punishment. The study finds that serious street youth offenders are immersed in a lifestyle where crime, drugs, and criminal peers feed off of one another isolating

---

59. Stephen Baron, Leslie Kennedy, *Deterrence and Homeless Male Street Youths*, 40 *Canadian Journal Crim*. (1998).

them from conventional society. The findings suggest that traditional models of deterrence must be re-examined when dealing with extremely "at risk" groups.

French sociologist and philosopher Emile Durkheim (1858-1917), identified what he referred to as "two laws which seem...to prevail in the evolution of the apparatus of punishment".[60] The first is the law of quantitative change, which is formulated by Durkheim as:

> The intensity of punishment is the greater the more closely societies approximate to a less developed type-and the more the central power assumes an absolute character.

The second law, which Durkheim refers to as the law of qualitative change, namely:

> Deprivations of liberty, and of liberty alone, varying in time according to the seriousness of the crime, tend to become more and more the normal means of social control.[61]

The two laws are, in reality, not two separate laws. Durkheim explains that the second law is merely a trend towards

---

60. *Philosophy of Punishment*, edited by Robert M. Baird and Stuart E. Rosenbaum. Article on: *Justice, Civilization, and the Death Penalty: Answering van den Haag*, J.H. Reiman, New York, Prometheus Books (1988), pp.109-124.
61. Worldwide web: http://www.relst.uiuc.edu/durkheim/

moderation of punishment referred to in the first law. The first law refers to two distinct trends, which usually coincide, but not always. Namely, that moderation of punishment accompanies both the movement from less to more advanced types of society and the movement from more to less absolute rule. Society and the rule are normally interlinked, but where they are not, the effect of one trend may offset the effect of the other. Thus, a primitive society without absolute rule may have milder punishments than an equally primitive but more absolutist society. Durkheim's precise claim is that punishment becomes less intense as societies become more advanced, which is of course a generalization that he takes support from pre-Christian times.

Professor Jerzy Sarnecki is the Head of the Department of Criminology at Stockholm University and the President of the Scandinavian Research Council for Criminology. He underlines that there are many theories regarding the "crimes committed by the poor."[62] "Where social control and systems are lacking and restraints and frustrations prevail, criminal offences may easily be the result. When human expectations are not met it may result in frustration. Theories that poverty is a cause of crime are many in the criminological research. One confirmation is the 1860s in Sweden, known as the famine year, where the crime rate grew enormously. A hungry stomach and social instability can easily break value systems".

62. Professor Sarnecki is originally from Poland where he was a student of Natural Science, till he came to Sweden and studied Sociology. My interview with him took place on February 16, 2005 in Stockholm.

"Contrastingly, what is interesting to note, is the phenomena of growth in GDP along with a growth in crime in some countries. In certain countries, welfare may lead to a growth of crime. Taking Sweden as an example, initially when the welfare growth took place there was a decline in the crime rate, however, later, in the 1920s a parallel growth between crime and welfare took place. There are two reasons for this, the first one is of course the better welfare the more temptations and resources to strive for, the second reason which may be of great importance to a State like India, is the reduction of informal social control mechanisms. Let me take, Japan as an example, where the crime rate is intact but the welfare growth increasing. Japan has maintained the informal social control, and not taken the western idea into the Japanese system. The Japanese set up is that of the old Japanese social system where the value system of old times is still kept parallel to a western welfare model. Thus, there is a stability maintained parallel to the growth of resources. The price paid for a western welfare system could be that of a growth in crime rates. This is not very complicated, if you look at Asia or the Mid East, you will see that the surrendering of rich cultural and social standards always lead to complications. Where the value systems are kept, namely, the role of elders, children and hierarchal structures are kept, less complications and frustrations occur".

4. State Responsibility

The capability approach suggested by Nobel Prize-winning welfare economist Dr. Amartya Sen provides a useful framework for understanding the intrinsic value of Economic, Social and Cultural rights (ESC rights). According to Dr. Sen, "the notion of capability is essentially one of freedom—the range of options a person has in deciding what kind of life to lead." He argues that economic poverty and deprivation should be seen in relation to their role in curtailing the freedom of a person to lead a life that s/he values. The freedom to live a normal span of life, for example, is curtailed by premature mortality, and the freedom to read or write is curtailed by illiteracy. Enjoyment of ESC rights enhances the freedom of individuals by increasing their capabilities and their quality of life.

Seeing poverty as a capability failure can lead to demands for appropriate social arrangements through placing obligations on states. This approach also provides a framework for judging policies by their impact on the enhancement of citizens' capabilities (whether or not the enhanced capability comes through the growth of real incomes). Finally, a capability approach can be a means for assessing the impact of discrimination based on factors such as race, class, caste and gender. Discrimination can, for example, constrain capability and thus the freedom of a person by denying him/her employment or appropriate medical care.

Dr. Sen identifies five ways in which education and health contribute to the freedom of a person:

1. Intrinsic Importance

   Being educated and healthy are valuable achievements in themselves, and the opportunity to have them can be of direct importance to a person's effective freedom.

2. Instrumental Personal Roles

   A person's education and health can help him or her to do many things—other than just being educated and healthy—that are valuable. They can, for instance, be important for getting a job and more generally for making use of economic opportunities. The resulting expansion in incomes and economic means can, in turn, add to a person's freedom to achieve functioning that he or she values.

3. Instrumental Social Roles

   Greater literacy and basic education can facilitate public discussion of social needs and encourage informed collective demands (e.g. for healthcare and social security); these, in turn, can help expand the facilities that the public enjoys, and contribute to the better utilization of available services.

4. Instrumental Process Roles

    The process of schooling can have benefits apart from its explicitly aimed objectives, namely formal education. Schooling also brings young people in touch with others and thereby broadens their horizons, and this can be particularly important for young girls.

5. Empowerment and Distributive Roles

    Greater literacy and educational achievements of disadvantaged groups can increase their ability to resist oppression, to organize politically, and to get a fairer deal.

The effects of education and health are not necessarily confined to the person who receives them:

> "Expansion of health and education can have influences that go much beyond the immediate personal effects. For example, one person's educational ability can be of use to another. The interpersonal connections can be of political significance as well; for example, a community may benefit generally from the civic attention it receives through the educated activism of a particular group within that community."

Dr. Sen also examines the role of food in fostering freedom:

> "The freedom that people enjoy to lead a decent life, including freedom from hunger, from avoidable morbidity, from premature mortality, etc., is quite centrally connected with the provision of food and related necessities. Also the compulsion to acquire enough food may force vulnerable people to do things, which they resent doing, and may make them accept lives with little freedom. The role of food in fostering freedom can be an extremely important one."

With regard to food policy, Dr. Sen distinguishes two kinds of perspectives—the instrumental perspective and the intrinsic perspective. The instrumental perspective emphasizes economic incentives for expansion of national output, including food production. Dr. Sen proposes that the instrumental perspective should not limit itself to advancing the freedom to earn profits, however. Other, broader kinds of freedoms such as freedom of information, assembly and opposition should also be advanced. These freedoms play a crucial role in the delivery and use of food. In the intrinsic perspective, according to Dr. Sen, freedom from hunger can be seen as having value in and of itself. Therefore, economic development and social progress should be assessed by examining whether they enhance basic positive freedoms to avoid premature mortality, to escape morbidity, to eliminate malnutrition, and so on.

> The importance of this perspective arises

> partly from the fact that the metrics of gross national product, real income, etc., may often be quite misleading about the extent of freedom that people do enjoy and can build their lives on. Even in such elementary matters as avoiding premature mortality, the statistics of national products (including those of food output) can hide more than they reveal. It is possible for the national product per head and the food availability per person to go up sharply without reducing mortality rates, sometimes accompanied by increased mortality.

Dr. Sen's arguments regarding food policy can be extended to social and economic policy (development policy) matters in general. They can be examined to assess whether they intrinsically enhance ESC rights and thereby the dignity and freedom of the individual. [63]

---

63. Amartya Sen, "Food and Freedom," *World Development* 17 (1989): p.769. Also see Jean Dreze and Amartya Sen, *India: Economic Development and Social Opportunity,* Delhi: Oxford India Paperbacks (1998), p. 11.

5. Social Welfare as a Legal Theory

A.W. Lundstedt, a Swedish legal theorist and lawmaker, was part of the Scandinavian Realist School of thought. For Lundstedt, legal theory was based on empirical social observation rather than value judgements.[64] He argued that once the observation of law has been freed from ideological and other distorting perceptions, it could be seen that legal activity must rest upon the supposition that it is "indispensable for the existence of society". This assumption may be criticized as being very ideological in itself. The foundation of Lundstedt's "constructive" investigation of the socially indispensable phenomenon of law was the concept of "social welfare".[65] This concept could only result in a real social fact.

Lundstedt explained that social welfare:

> "...involves certain *actual* evaluations of that which is the best for the society concerning the enactment of a law...or concerning interpretation of a certain law or finally concerning...some maxim when an immediately applicable law is lacking...In general the matter can be expressed thus: socially useful is that which is actually evaluated as a social interest." [66]

---

64. Hilaire McCoubrey and Nigel D. White, *Textbook on Jurisprudence*, second edition, London, Blackstone Press Limted (1996), pp.173-175.
65. A.V. Lundstedt, *Legal Thinking Revised*, Stockholm, Almqvist & Wiksell (1956), pp. 132-136.
66. Ibid., p.137.

Lundstedt cautioned against unequal distribution, and emphasized the beneficial consequences for the community as a whole. However, an important consideration of his was the psychological importance of a common sense of justice in the operation of law. Lundstedt treated this sense of justice, in effect, as an appreciation of coincidence with the interests embodied in social welfare. However, this is a very simplified "people-friendly" notion of justice, but, nevertheless, carries the functioning of law, which is social welfare, much faster and much closer to the understanding of the common man and the lawmaker.

The states which have abolished the capital punishment have mostly been recognized as strong welfare states as well. One commonality between the countries which have abolished this punishment is that they have a prominent welfare agenda for their citizens. Hence, given the crucial argument for a strong welfare state, adding the responsibilities of a welfare state towards its citizens, it becomes a must that the reasons for imposing a punishment must relate, not to the criminal, but to the crime. Justice A.S. Anand observed in a case: "It's the nature and gravity of the crime but not the criminal, which are germane for consideration of appropriate punishment in a criminal trial."

The State's support and execution of capital punishment exacerbates some of the most troubling aspects of the Indian condition. Capital punishment provides a seemingly simple solution to complex problems, encouraging our society to focus compulsively on fixing individual responsibility and apportioning blame. Moreover, part of what is at stake in the contemporary politics of capital punishment is a contest to claim the status of the victim. Today, this label is widely appropriated, and used by persons accused of capital crimes to explain what they did and why they did it as well as by the so-called victims' rights movement to claim that the only real victims are those innocent citizens whose lives are tragically ended by capital crimes. Instead of the difficult, often frustrating work of understanding what in our society breeds such heinous acts of violence, state killing offers all of us a way out. Those acts are "their" fault, not our problem. The world can and should be understood in a set of clear typologies of good and evil, victim and villain. State killing depends on flattened narratives of criminal or personal responsibility of the type found in melodrama and responds to insistent demands that we use punishment to restore clarity to the moral order.

As Harvard Law professor Martha Minow argues, the struggle over "blame.... obscures the complex interactions of individual choice, social structures, and the historical obstacles within which both individuals and institutions operate. As a result, public debate, legal solutions, and political talk neglect the complex solutions needed to sustain and equip victimized individuals to choose differently while also restricting the individuals and social forces that oppress them." This is not to say that responsibility and blame should not be assigned; but state killing, by responding to and encouraging a yearning for a world without moral ambiguity, does not make us safer or our society healthier. Capital punishment certainly distracts. It encourages the quest for revenge rather than efforts at reconciliation and social reconstruction. "Capital punishments", Benjamin Rush once observed, "are the natural offspring of monarchical governments.... An execution in a republic is like a human sacrifice in a religion." Along with the right to make war, the death penalty is the ultimate measure of sovereignty and the ultimate test of political power. With the transition from monarchical to democratic regimes, one might have thought that such a vestige of monarchical power would have no place in a democracy and, as a result, would wither away. Yet, at least in India, which purports to be the most democratic of democratic nations, it persists with a vengeance. This contradiction is damaging the notion of justice in the country. Dr. Amartya Sen's capability failure is undoubtedly linked to the responsibility of the State.

It is difficult to dissent from Lundstedt's legal theory that a concept of social welfare should involve an evaluation of the welfare of society. This seems unavoidable and that such evaluations should be actual seems to be very desirable. It is required if social welfare is to be accepted as a means of understanding the operation of law as a real phenomenon. However, most crucial to remember is the added burden of welfare for a state, where economic disparities are greater than a balanced distribution of state resources. This added burden cannot be compensated with greater punishments. The law will have no contradictions,if the aim—justice based on social justice—is taken care of.

This can be achieved through a court of law with inquisitorial capacity. In the context of a Welfare State, the court must be understood to be an important part of the state machinery. Dr. Sen's capability approach must be understood as a direct link to the State's responsibility to put social justice in operation. The enjoyment of economic, social and cultural rights enhances the freedom of individuals by increasing their capabilities and their quality of life, according to Dr. Sen. Thus, a capability failure, meaning a failure of providing such rights, should by no means be compensated by harsher penal systems. Harsher penal systems cannot provide the framework for judging policies by their impact on the enhancement of citizens' capabilities, whether or not the enhanced capability comes through the growth of real incomes. However, a sense of responsibility for such failures can be provided by a framework such as suggested by Dr. Sen.

6. The Psycho-legal Field

Important Definitions

The application of psychology and law can be differentiated in terms of psychology in law; psychology and law; and psychology of law. According to Blackburn, psychology in law refers to specific applications of psychology within law, such as the reliability of eyewitness testimony, mental state of the defendant, and a parent's suitability for child custody in divorce cases. Psychology and law are used to denote psycho-legal research into offenders, lawyers, magistrates, judges, and jurors. Finally, psychology of law refers to psychological research into such issues as to why people obey/disobey certain laws, moral development and public perceptions and attitudes towards various penal sanctions. The term forensic psychology should according, to Blackburn, only be used to denote the "direct provision of psychological information to the courts, that is, psychology in the courts".[67]

Forensics or forensic science is the application of science to questions which are of interest to the legal system. Forensic evidence consists of anything that can be used in a court of law to convict a person of a crime. There are many tools that can be used to gather evidence and most require a meticulous approach to collection so that the evidence is not compromised. Many things that seem unusual or are easily overlooked can produce valuable

67. R. Blackburn, 'What is Forensic Psychology?' *Legal and Criminological Psychology* (1996), pp. 3-16.

evidence, such as insects, or even the way that a crime scene is laid out. There are also numerous techniques and chemicals used to gather evidence.

Many experts divide forensic psychology into two standards:

1. Applying psychological techniques to help in the prosecution of criminals
2. The rehabilitation of criminals once in the prison system[68]

Punishment: Psychological Understanding

> When pocket-picking was punishable by hanging, in England, the crowds that gathered about the gallows to enjoy the spectacle of an execution were particularly likely to have their pockets picked by skilful operators who, to say the least, were not deterred by the exhibition of "justice".[69]

---

68. Separate Investigative Psychology (IP), created by Professor David Canter, who has written books *Criminal Shadows* and *Mapping Murder*. IP is not a form of profiling *per se*, but is a means by which scientific knowledge can provide resources that can be used in police investigations. Professor Canter has been asked to provide "profiles" of criminals for the police, but these are based on scientific evaluations, rather than any experience-based procedures. IP began after Prof. Canter was asked to aid the police in the investigation of the Railway Rapist case in the late 1980s in the UK.

69. *Philosophy of Punishment*, edited by Robert M. Baird and Stuart E. Rosenbaum, New York, Prometheus Books (1988), p.48.

Operant conditioning, as named by psychologist B.F. Skinner, is the modification of behaviour, namely the actions of animals, which are brought about by the consequences that follow upon the occurrence of the behaviour. In simple terms, behaviour operates on the environment producing various effects.[70] The phrase operant conditioning draws out a crucial distinction from Pavlovian conditioning, which Skinner termed respondent—respondent conditioning, like a dog's salivation or a kneejerk, has neither much effect on the environment, nor is its occurrence changed by its effectiveness or ineffectiveness in the environment. These two types of conditioning are also distinguished since they are conceptually different. As their names imply—operant conditioning is explained by its consequences, that is, functionally; while respondent conditioning is explained by its antecedents, which is causally. In operant conditioning, punishment is the presentation of a stimulus contingent on a response, which results in a decrease in response strength, and as evidenced by a decrease in the frequency of response. The effectiveness of punishment in suppressing the response is dependent on many factors, including the intensity of the stimulus, and the consistency with which the stimulus is presented when the response occurs. Important to note is that in parenting, additional factors that increase the effectiveness of punishments include a verbal explanation of the reason for the punishment and a good relationship between the parent

70. Ilham Dilman, *Mind, Brain and Behaviour: Discussions of B.F. Skinner and J.R. Searle*, London, Routledge (1988).

and the child. Punishment may be divided into two types: Positive punishment is the application of an aversive stimulus. Negative punishment is the removal of a desired condition. [71]

Definition. Behaviourism is an approach to psychology based on the proposition that behaviour is interesting and worthy of scientific research. Within that broad approach, there are different emphases. Some behaviourists argue that the observation of behaviour is the best or most convenient way of investigating psychological and mental processes. Others believe that it is, in fact, the only way of investigating such processes, while still others argue that behaviour itself is the only appropriate subject of psychology, and that common psychological terms (belief, goals, etc.) have no referents and/or only refer to behaviour. Those taking this point of view sometimes refer to their field of study as behaviour analysis or behavioural science, rather than psychology.

Does substantive criminal law, which distributes criminal liability and punishment, deter? Behavioural science data, in short, negates this question. The claim here is not that criminal law never influences behaviour, but that conditions of influence vary and are not at all typical. Contrastingly, adjudicators and lawmakers assume that rules always influence conduct. This assumption holds serious consequences for the administration of justice.

---

71. B.F. Skinner, *Science and Human Behaviour*. New York , Macmillan, cop. (1953).

Deterrence and Psychology

In another study from 2002, the actual criminal's knowledge of the penalties assigned by criminal codes was measured.[72] Anderson tested males who had been imprisoned for a felony, persons who, given their time in prison and their interest in the question, one would assume had the motivation and the opportunity to learn the various and comparative magnitudes of sentences.[73] Twenty-two per cent of the criminals thought they knew exactly what the punishment would be for the crime they committed, 18 per cent reported that they had no idea of the penalty, or that they knew but were wrong, and 35 per cent reported that, as to the punishment for the offence they committed– "I didn't even think about it".

What is important to understand is that a potential offender

72. See, David Andersson, 'The Deterrence Hypothesis and Picking Pockets at the Pickpocket's Hanging', *American Law and Economic Rev.* (2002), p. 295.
73. A felony, in many common law legal systems, is the term for a "very serious" crime; misdemeanours are considered to be less serious. Crimes which are commonly considered to be felonies include: aggravated assault, arson, burglary, murder, and rape. Those who are convicted of a felony are known as felons. Originally, felonies were crimes for which the punishment was either death or forfeiture of property. Nowadays, felons can receive punishments which range in severity; from probation, to imprisonment, to execution. Felons often receive additional punishments such as the loss of voting rights, exclusion from certain lines of work, and loss of firearm rights. In addition, some states consider a felony conviction to be grounds for an uncontested divorce.

need not understand law in an intellectual sense in order to be influenced by the same. A perceived threat even deter rats. They react to conditions that they experience, for instance, electric shocks when they approach and pull a mechanism which had previously given them food. Similarly, potential offenders may have limited knowledge or no knowledge of the law *per se*, yet, due to their own experience, or that of someone else, indirectly or subconsciously they come to understand the conditions of liability or punishment that Criminal Law sets out. Policing practise may be a good example. When a potential offender sees four times as many police cars passing by his neighbourhood, he may perceive a greater risk breaking into somebody's home. What is crucial to understand is whether the same thinking process can be applied when the discussion entails the effective communication of the substantive Criminal Law rule that lawmakers have justified on the basis of the deterrence theory? It seems improbable due to the fact that criminal laws are not in their application a contemporaneous or common event, as compared to police cars passing by.[74] It seems highly unrealistic to conclude that a potential offender can make, as the rat could, an intuitive multiple-regression analysis to divine the applicable liability rule and its meaning for him. Police efficiency, judicial sentencing discretion, and a variety of prosecutorial practices and policies, are all factors influencing the criminal mind.

74. The examples are inspired by a working paper by Paul Robinson, *Does Criminal Law Deter? A Behavioural Science Investigation*, Paper 32, The Berkeley Electronic Press (2004).

An effective deterrent system would not impose imprisonment, and certainly not the same term of imprisonment, for every rule violation it wished to deter. First, it would not be cost-effective. The societal harm of only some offences can justify the high costs of this punishment. More importantly, an effective deterrent system must modulate its punishment to achieve its programme. For instance, it may want to tie the amount of punishment to the degree of seriousness of the offence so as to provide a continuing disincentive for offenders to commit a more serious offence. That is, if rape automatically triggered the most serious penalty, every rapist would have nothing to lose and something to gain, eliminating the primary witness—killing his victim. Furthermore, there is a range of other factors, from difficulty of detection, to level of publicity, which an efficient deterrence system would want to take into account in setting the optimum level of punishment.

The studies relating to punishment amount suggest both greater complexity than current deterrence analysis seems to comprehend and dynamics inconsistent with modern deterrence practices. The first finding, of the relevant animal studies is unremarkable: the degree to which the administration of punishment suppresses later actions that the animal had previously been reinforced for taking, depends heavily on the amount of the punishment. In one study in which the punishment consisted of electric shocks delivered immediately after the animal pressed a bar, an action that had previously led to rewards, the punishment hardly suppressed later bar pressings as if the shocks were mild in intensity. However, a great deal of behaviour suppression was achieved, close to complete suppression, if the shocks were of very high in intensity.[75] It is important to remember that the punishment is delivered immediately and after each and every 'transgressive' response, a set of conditions that are not likely to be achieved in instances of human criminal transgressions.

In a second study there is an interesting "adaptation to intensity" effect. In one study a pigeon was shocked for pecking a key that had previously delivered and continued to deliver a reward.[76] A shock level of 80 volts produced total response suppression when administered as punishment for the animal's first response. When the shock level was slightly below that, at 60 volts, it had little behaviour suppression effect. However, if the shock level started at the undeterring 60 volts, then was gradually increased, the pigeons continued with the punished response, even up to 300 volts, far beyond the 80 volt complete deterrence level. The application of this to punishments within the criminal justice system is unsettling, since it is often the case that the punishment for first offences is rather low, frequently consisting of short sentences, probation, or suspended sentences. This suggests that they may inadvertently be creating offenders who, like

75. See, E. Boe and Russell Church, Permanent Effects of Punishment during Extinction, 63 *Journal of Comparative & Physiological Psychology* (1967), p. 486.

76. See, Azran, Holz and Hake, op.cit.

the pigeon, learn to tolerate punishment levels that, if administered earlier, would have deterred the punished action. The data regarding sentences for first offenders, and particularly young offenders, suggests that the problem may be a real one. Forty-five per cent of all felony offenders without a prior conviction are not given an incarcerate sentence.[77] Sixty-six per cent of all felony offenders in the US under the age of 20 are sentenced to probation..

Furthermore, in the US, news about a youthful offender who has committed some horribly violent offence and who does receive a prison sentence is covered widely. The news coverage is probably a testimony to how rare it is to sentence young offenders to prison.

From several perspectives, this is an acceptable, even good, outcome: judges often do not send youthful offenders to prison because the experience may increase their future likelihood of committing criminal offences.[78] They may also experience appalling treatment by older convicts. However, from the deterrence perspective, it may bring about the 'hardening to punishment' effect observed in animals, in which an escalating series of punishments, if it begins at a level that is ineffective in controlling the initial transgression simply conditions the person to tolerate the

---

77. Bureau of Justice Statistics, US Department of Justice, *Felony Defendants in Large Urban Counties*, Table 35 (1998).
78. Zvi Eisikovits and Michael Baizerman, 'Doing Time: Violent Youth in a Juvenile Facility and in an Adult Prison,' 6 *Journal of Official Counselling Services & Rehabilitation* (1982), p. 5.

increasing punishments without reducing the rate of transgressions.

The Potential Offender and the Rational Choice

If the potential offender does have the knowledge, will he bring this understanding to affect his conduct, when he makes a choice?

The study of decision-making patterns of people conducted by behavioural scientists indicates that being able to demonstrate that a person has some knowledge of various facts that could be relevant to a decision does not mean that those facts are recalled, and mobilized appropriately by the decision-maker. Much depends on the momentary context in which the need for the decision arises or on the particular interpretations that the decision-maker puts on the facts, as they are relevant to him.[79] Rational decision-making about criminal activities becomes difficult due to the particular personality of the crime-prone actor and the circumstances in which the decisions arise. Data suggests that potential offenders as a group are people who are less inclined to think at all about the consequences and effects of their criminal conduct. Their behaviour is often risk-seeking rather than risk-avoiding, and tends to be more impulsive than the average.[80] There are a number of

79. See, Lee Ross and Richard Nisbett, *The Person and the Situation: Perspectives of Social Psychology* (1991).
80. See, David P. Farrington, *Human Development and Criminal Careers*, in *Oxford Handbook of Criminology*, 2nd edition (1997), pp. 361-384.

temporary states of mind that are likely to drive out rational considerations of punishment, such as desire for revenge or retaliation, and suddenly induced rage and or anger, the duration of which can extend from minutes to days.[81] Certain states of mind can be of a longer duration, and can induce flawed reasoning. Paranoia, feelings that the surroundings are an immediate and acute threat, can be ongoing for months. When it is acute it is likely that the degree of threat felt will take over considerations of any deterrence of possible punishment. Manic depression, which occurs when the manic-depressive cycles are into the manic phase, and can give the person experiencing it a feeling of incredible brilliance, which is likely to cause him to underestimate the likelihood of not-so-brilliant forces of law ever catching and convicting him.[82]

What is essential to understand is that these are examples of diagnosable mental difficulties. However, there are many personality differences which are not regarded as "mental illnesses", yet they have an impact on the deterrence effect at the moment a person is contemplating a crime. There will be a constant effect on the behaviour of the individual provided that these characteristics are permanent and continuously displayed. For instance, many people may be characterized by a low ability to delay gratification, and they are less likely to give in to temptation in the present.[83]

---

81. See, Ronald Comer, *Abnormal Psychology*, 3rd edition (1998).
82. See, Ronald Comer, op.cit., pp. 262-265.
83. See, Janet Metcalfe and Walter Mischel, 'A Hot/Cool System Analysis of Delay of Gratification: Dynamics of Willpower,' 106 *Psychology Review 3* (1999).

Gottfredson and Hirschi, in *A General Theory of Crime* (1990), point out that the typical criminal is characterized by many non-criminal signs of absence of self-control, and commits a "wide variety of criminal acts, with no strong inclination to pursue a specific criminal act or a pattern of criminal acts to the exclusion of others". They conclude that "people who lack self-control will tend to be impulsive, intensive, physical (as opposed to mental), risk-taking, short sighted, and they will tend therefore to engage in criminal and analogous acts". Even when mental abnormalities that distort reasoning are absent, both the ability and the motivation to make the calculations required for deterrence can be influenced by a variety of contextual effects.

To conclude, even if one had instant familiarity with detailed rules, their application depends on the actor's resolution of factual issues that may be difficult, if not impossible, in the split second in which the actor has to make a decision which could either be offensive or defensive. It is difficult to fit this to the image of a person who is affected by complex rational deterrence considerations. A further gap between reality and the assumption of legal rule influence on conduct is the unrealistic extent to which lawmakers think they can micromanage conduct. This is an immensely risky approach, denying and overlooking crucial data which could explain reasons for crime and for becoming a criminal. Moreover, the deterrence approach minimizes scientific solutions to cure illnesses in society, and maximizes a judgemental view against the offender.

7. The Social Chain

State Responsibility. It is only logical to assume that in states where inequality in distribution of income and wealth is immense, and socio-economic rights dysfunctional, it is highly questionable when the state steps in to assume responsibility at the point of punishment alone. Furthermore, my right to life entails that you have a duty not to kill me. If I have a right to welfare as a citizen of a Welfare State, who is obliged to respect it and what must they do? If the bearers and nature of the obligation cannot be identified, the correlation between rights and duties will fail, and the attempt to establish the claims related to a welfare set-up fails.[84] Is this the case when capital punishment is applied in a Welfare State such as India? Let us examine this question after examining the following example:

Free Mind Exercise

Ganga Ram, known as Gangu, is 32-years-old and has been sentenced to death for the rape and callous murder of his victim, 14-year-old Sonia. The judgement described the act as heinous and so brutal that only the death sentence would touch the consciousness of people like Ganga Ram. The prosecutor described him as cold-blooded and distant

---

84. In *Eternal Values for a Changing* Society by Swami Ranganathananda (1971), 3rd edition, p. 693, the pragmatic philosopher had in a speech advised the young Indian Administrative Officers, stating under the heading "The Administrator in a Welfare State" that the State in a democratic society derives its strength from the coordinated wills of all its free and equal citizens. In the absence of this strength, the State becomes an imposition on the people.

from any human emotion, a person dangerous to society. Gangu belongs to a village called Sikandarpur, situated north of Bihar. He is the only son of Hari and Lakshmi. When Gangu was five-years-old, Hari lost his job in a post office were he had worked as a tea-boy for five years. The reason for ending Hari's employment was his health. Hari had constant asthma attacks. This resulted in the discontinuation of Gangu's schooling. Hari started drinking and became completely incapable of working. Hari also started beating both Gangu and Lakshmi every day. Gangu, as a six-year-old, witnessed and experienced not only the daily abuse of his mother and of himself, but also the horrendous sight of his mother being raped by one of his father's drinking partners, Sonu. When the incident took place, Gangu was beaten and tied to a heavy stool.

The incident made Gangu an introvert and very lonely. Lakshmi took up a temporary job as a cleaner, and Gangu, now seven, started working in a warehouse. Gangu's boss, Abraham, was always dissatisfied with the work of the children in the warehouse and used to beat them with leather belts and sometimes call them into his room to abuse them. Gangu ran away from the warehouse after his first beating and took a job as a tea-boy in a private office. Here Gangu remained only three days–after being accused of stealing money, he was heavily beaten by two men.

Two years later, Hari died, and the life of Gangu and Lakshmi became even more hell-like when Hari's friend

Sonu again entered their home, this time with two other drunk men. Gangu, all of nine years, is severely abused and his mother locked and abused for several days.

Till the age of 32, Gangu lived as an introvert. One afternoon in June, Gangu was standing next to his cycle-rickshaw watching Sonia coming back from school. As usual, Gangu's eyes were blank and he had no expression on his face. Sonia asked Gangu whether he could drop her to her house. Gangu nodded, but took off track to a deserted place and brutally raped the young girl. Sonia was still conscious when Gangu took up a stone and banged it several times on her head. He then strangled her. After killing her, Gangu went back to his rickshaw and kept staring at nothing with his blank look.

Is this incident a matter of one case/situation/life-story?

This is one exercise of the many so-called *Free Mind Exercises* conducted by me during various Human Rights trainings around India with students of law, psychology, sociology and teachers training students. Students are not bound to the various frameworks of their respective discipline, hence the exercise is called *Free Mind.* The aim is to create a societal understanding where the students are given broad guidelines namely, to remove judgementalism from their approach, and not to justify crime at any point. The highlight of socio-economic conditions in the country makes the students understand the Social Chain, where the causes of frustrations are discussed along with the state's role in the whole situation. Conclusions are mostly based on the crime and not the criminal. However, it is imperative to note that the conclusions regarding Gangaram's punishment changes depending on how much information on the socio-economic conditions is with the students. Whenever the crime alone was described, the students would opt for capital punishment, a clear indication that the moment the background of conditions is looked into, a sense of common responsibility occurs and the application of capital punishment diminishes.

In *Excel Wear vs Union of India*, one of the judges underlined that the word "life" in Article A1 of the Constitution does not mean mere animal existence.[85] Furthermore, the right visualized by this article is to live a dignified life. In the context of state responsibility, it is important to understand that the right in Article 21 must be one of the duties of the state and a court of law.

85. AIR 1979 SC 25.

8. Children in India: Facts and Figures[86]

- There are 4 lakh child prostitutes in the country. It is said that about 200 girls and women enter prostitution daily.
- Forty-five per cent of the children in the 6-14 year age group are out of school.
- About 11 million children live on the streets.
- About 15,000 children are reported missing every year.
- 400 infant girls are killed annually.
- 20,000 female foetuses are aborted every year.
- Nearly half the births remain unregistered.
- One-fourth of India's 1 billion population is comprised of children below 18 years.
- Estimates suggest between 11.28 to 100 million children are in the workforce.

In India, 47 per cent of children in the age group of 0 to 3 years are undernourished, 51 per cent suffer from severe or moderate anaemia and child mortality (0 to 5 years) is the highest in the world. In these circumstances the Integrated Child Development Scheme (ICDS) is the only hope for children in the age group of 0 to 6 years.

86. Worldwide web: http://www.childrensrightsindia.org/cact/cact.htm

The allocation for ICDS in 2005 increased from Rs. 1,490.40 crores to Rs. 3,142.25 crore. This seems to be a huge increment; it is still not sufficient to cover the required cost of universal coverage of all 17 lakh habitations in India, the centre points out. Further, supplementary nutrition is currently provided to 3.4151 crore children, as opposed to 16 crore children (47 per cent of whom are undernourished) in the 0-6 age group. The coverage of settlements is also highly inadequate, there are only 6.412 lakh anganwadis in the country, compared with an estimated 17 lakh required for universal coverage based on existing norms. To implement the Supreme Court's order in letter and spirit, the allocation should have been increased six-fold, but it has gone up by only 2 per cent. In India there are about 1.25 crore child labour, 4 lakh child prostitutes and 1.13 crore street children (in six metropolitan cities). Despite this there is rarely any special attention paid to children in difficult circumstances.

However, the continued existence of child labour, many of whom are also children out of school, is a contradiction to the fundamental right to free and compulsory education. The budget estimates for NCLP schools, which cater to only those child workers rescued from "hazardous labour" was only Rs. 125.05 crore.[87]

87. Source: *The Hindu*, 'Budgetary Allocation for Child Welfare Inadequate', Sunday, March 13, 2005.

9. Empathy: A Form of Social Awareness

We expect our judges to be almost superhuman in wisdom, in propriety, in decorum and in humanity. There must be no other group in society, which must fulfil this standard of public expectation...

Gerald Gall,
The Canadian Legal System[88]

This is how empathy is defined in *Psychology : An Introduction* (Ninth Edition) by
Charles G. Morris, Prentice Hall (1996):

"Closely related to the ability to read other people's emotions is empathy—the arousal of an emotion in an observer that is a vicarious response to the other person's situation... Empathy depends not only on one's ability to identify someone else's emotions but also on one's capacity to put oneself in the other person's place and to experience an appropriate emotional response. Just as sensitivity to non-verbal cues increases with age, so does empathy: The cognitive and perceptual abilities required for empathy develop only as a child matures..." (page 442)

"In empathy training, for example, each member of the couple is taught to share inner feelings and to listen to and

88. *The Canadian Legal System*, 4th edn, Carswell, Calgary (1995).

understand the partner's feelings before responding to them. The empathy technique focuses the couple's attention on feelings and requires that they spend more time listening and less time in rebuttal." (page 576).

Empathy according to the *Encyclopaedia Britannica* (1999 Edition) is:

"Empathy *and other forms of social awareness* are important in the development of a moral sense. Morality embraces a person's beliefs about the appropriateness or goodness of what he does, thinks, or feels... Childhood is ... the time at which moral standards begin to develop in a process that often extends well into adulthood. The American psychologist Lawrence Kohlberg hypothesized that people's development of moral standards passes through stages that can be grouped into three moral levels...

At the third level, that of post-conventional moral reasoning, the adult bases his moral standards on principles that he himself has evaluated and that he accepts as inherently valid, regardless of society's opinion. He is aware of the arbitrary, subjective nature of social standards and rules, which he regards as relative rather than absolute in authority.

Thus the bases for justifying moral standards pass from avoidance of punishment to avoidance of adult disapproval and rejection to avoidance of internal guilt and self-recrimination. The person's moral reasoning also moves towards increasingly greater social scope (i.e. including more people and institutions) and greater abstraction (i.e. from reasoning about physical events such as pain or pleasure to reasoning about values, rights, and implicit contracts)."

This need not affect the independence of a judge. However, having empathy as a minimal for a judge may increase the ability to produce effective remedies for children, and would surely increase the psychological understanding and capacity of a judge.

Bringing Social Disparities to the Court of Law

Advocate Ashok Agarwal, the founder of Social Jurist, a civil rights group fighting child labour through legal intervention, explains that rehabilitation becomes a far-fetched argument when a basic understanding of deprived children's situation is lacking.[89] Agarwal elaborates his statement by referring to a case after the Delhi High Court decision of January 20, 2004, followed by the Delhi Government order of April 27, 2004, directing the public schools of Delhi to give admission and freeship to the extent of 25-20 per cent to children belonging to the weaker sections. Many public schools invented ways and means to frustrate both the High Court and the government.[90] A public school built on public land, having reluctantly

89. Worldwide web: http://www.socialjurist.com/
90. Meeting with Mr. Ashok Agarwal took place on August 11, 2005, in New Delhi High Court.

admitted only 10 students from the weaker sections in the academic year 2004-05, issued a circular to the parents of the 10 students, informing them that a decision has been taken by the school managing committee that the proof of family income, duly issued by the competent authority, should be submitted every year; and asked them to submit a fresh proof of income certificate by the SDM.[91] Public schools have no authority to devise their own admission criteria for students falling under the weaker-sections quota. Rule 145 of the Delhi School Education Rules, 1973, which empowers the head of every recognized school to regulate admission to a recognized unaided school or to any class thereof (either on the basis of admission test or on the basis of result in a particular class or school), has no application at all to the admission of students falling under the weaker-sections quota.

Agarwal explains that in order to make the judge "connect" with the situation of destitutes, he brought 25 destitute children to the court room, and made the Director of Education, Government of Delhi, ask the Bench whether he as a destitute child was guaranteed an absolute right to education. Agarwal's methodology is based on creating empathy within the court of law for sections distant from the Bench's reality.

91. Ashok Agarwal, *The Tribune*, Tuesday, May 17, 2005, Chandigarh, India.

10. The Right to Life and the Administration of Justice

Professor Ronald Dworkin of Oxford University developed a sophisticated view of judicial decision-making, based on democracy, arguing strongly for individual and minority rights, which could not be overridden by the legislature on simple policy grounds.[92] His theory has been understood as anti-utilitarian, where the majority should not be able to step on the minority's legal rights. This theory of democracy is linked to. Dworkin's view of the judicial process as the idea that judges act as protectors of individual rights against the State as well as between individuals. However, in States where basic needs are guaranteed but not enforced, such as less developed states as India, the anti-utilitarian view is not applicable.[93] In India in fact, it is a matter of the common good, where the Dworkin''s theory of justice, actually affects the majority of Indians.

Imagine believing that justice is something unreal and far from one's existence, imagine not knowing where to

---

92. See, Hilaire McCoubrey, Nigel D. White, *Textbook on Jurisprudence*, 2nd edition, Blackstone Press Limited (1996), p. 146.
93. On December 11, 1963, Jawaharlal Nehru made the following speech in the Lok Sabha: *One thing that distresses me very greatly is that, although I am convinced that the great majority of our population have bettered their economic condition a little, with more calories and more clothes, yet, there is a good number of people in India who have not profited by planning, and whose poverty is abysmal and most painful. I do think that some method should be found to remedy the situation.*

go when your rights are violated. This is a reality for mainstream Indians. The Legal Services Authorities Act, 1987, spells out "to constitute legal services authorities to provide free and competent legal services to the weaker sections of society to ensure that opportunities for securing justice are not denied to any citizen by reason of economic or other disabilities..." The Act envisages a nationwide network for legal aid and assistance. However, this textual effort to provide equal justice to all is so distant from realities, which our socially deprived Indian is suffering of. The majority of First Information Reports (FIR) of atrocities against Schedule Castes and Schedule Tribes are not reported as a result of non-accessibility to justice and discrimination against the poor. Similarly, some law groups claim that 70 per cent of the country's undertrials receive no legal representation—and half of them are locked in for petty cases. The faith of most of these undertrials was decided the day they were born into deprived socio-economic conditions. In *D. K. Basu vs State of West Bengal*, it was stated that not providing legal aid to persons who need it is a calculated assault on human dignity, and whenever human dignity is wounded, civilization takes a step backward—the flag of humanity must on each occasion fly half-mast.[94] Legal representation should be given to every person, because it is his right to have a legal say in the administration of justice.

---

94. (1997) 1 SCC 416, and AIR 1997 SC 610.

Undertrial in jail for 33 years

Fatehpur (UP): In another case of delayed justice, an undertrial has been languishing in a prison in Uttar Pradesh for over 33 years with both the complainant and witnesses in the case having died. Devi Prasad, a resident of Gazipur township in the district, was arrested and lodged as an undertrial for allegedly murdering his wife in 1973, police sources said. He was later shifted to the Varanasi jail and his family had also given him up for dead, the sources said. However, his brother Pitambar, who got information that Mr. Prasad was lodged in jail, met him recently, though the latter failed to recognize his relative. "He was 24 when he was jailed and today he is neither mentally or physically fit after spending almost his entire life behind bars," Mr. Pitambar said.– PTI
Source: *The Hindu*, Sunday, March 19, 2006

Access to justice for a person in need of legal representation fails at the initial stage itself. The immensely low fees of the legal aid lawyer triggers a legal process based on non-application of mind in dealing with a poor person's case in a just and fair manner. The fee of a legal aid lawyer could be anything between Rs 300 to -700 per case (7-15 USD), a case which could go on and on for time unlimited. The issue of delay of payment to legal aid lawyers is another put-off factor for lawyers not to opt for legal aid services. Mostly, the assistance of legal aid is delayed. However the law provides for legal aid at the point of arrest and has to ideally be notified within 24 hours. A public prosecutor, however, receives a salary from the government, and a sum of a couple of hundred rupees per day.

Norms for appointing lawyers for this purpose should be uniform and based on specialized skills. The preference of the aggrieved persons should be taken into consideration while determining the appointment of lawyers. Discussing the moral responsibilities within the profession of law becomes very difficult and far-fetched when the state differentiates between one category of lawyer from the other. The whole notion of the legal profession being a noble one and a branch of social service, are only notions, which will slowly die out due to this differentiation. Furthermore, it would reduce a number of lawyers sensitized to work with issues of human rights, legal aid and the poor. In Hoskot's case, various guidelines relating to legal aid have been given. The court in this case stated that junior lawyers should not be appointed, implying the importance of good and experienced lawyers. [95] Reasonable remuneration to lawyers in order to encourage seriousness, is a must. Whether Rs 300–700 is a reasonable remuneration needs to be scrutinized by the court of law.

The Legal Services Authority, in its "efforts" to spread the message of free legal aid to the masses, has completely overlooked the question of how to reach out to the needy. Legal Aid camps are held everywhere but in the interior of the country where the need is most, and the language

95. (1978) 3 SCC 544.

so complicated that even if justice is communicated to a small portion of the needy, it is not understood. The duty cast upon the state is beyond making the provision for legal aid for all, and beyond making legal aid a fundamental right in the law books. Legislation is merely a means, not the goal. Legislation meant for the poor has to have strategies and guarantees which brings the "messenger of rights", in this case the legal aid authorities, closer to the poor. One way of obtaining this would be through closer cooperation between the Legal Services Authorities and Civil Society and NGOs. India has succeeded in creating a force of volunteer lawyers, struggling to provide free legal aid to people in need. Here, legal aid services carry the same quality of casework as in any case handled by a lawyer. Correspondingly, strategies of how to reach out to the poor masses have developed far ahead of what the state has been able to achieve. In such a set up, where governmental legal aid clinics are falling apart, and where the appointment of lawyers with no interest and expertise in social justice issues is a commonality, only an organized form of collaboration between Civil Society groups and the Legal Services Authority could provide a somewhat complete access to justice for the socially deprived.

Indian conditions for investigation of crimes and trial court procedures in homicide cases do not inspire confidence. Methods of investigation remain crude, archaic and unscientific. Conviction is largely based on oral evidence of witnesses. Witnesses are often motivated by caste, communal and factional factors. It is not uncommon for the police to fabricate a case for caste or communal reasons or for the enemies of the accused to fabricate a case against him. Prosecutors are not trained to shun irrelevant considerations. Such factors may create an apparent cast-iron prosecution case but the reality may be different—an innocent man may have been the victim of a faulty or false prosecution.

Unfair administration of justice, along with an unrealistic view of access to justice, leads to dreadful results where, for instance, capital punishment is given, and the state has appointed a legal aid lawyer. The inflicted disproportionately of capital punishment on the poor and minorities often lead to a lesser quality in casework -putting justice and a person's life at risk.[96] Another very interesting issue involving the dilemma of capital punishment is the very impressive interpretation of Article 14, the Right to Equality, in the Indian Constitution. It consists of equality before the law, that is to say, equal protection of laws. In India, it is debated that the sentence of death violates Article 14 , which states equality in all senses. Article 14 is the article prohibiting legislative arbitrariness.

An "Untouchable" Justice System for the Poor

Article 17 of the Indian Constitution abolishes the practice of Untouchability and punishes the enforcement of any disability arising out of the practice. In order to enforce the Constitutional

96. Parul Sharma, "Access to Justice: A Farce", Combat Law; *Human Rights Magazine*, November-December 2004.

provisions, the Untouchability Offences Act, 1955, was passed by Parliament to make provisions for punishments for offences that amounted to observance of Untouchability in any form. The law was made even more stringent through an amendment, and it was renamed as the Protection of Civil Rights Act, 1955, under which the practice of Untouchability has been made an offence both cognizable and non-cognizable. However, convictions under this Act have been very few. Even where the cases ended in conviction, the punishment has been negligible according to many Human Rights lawyers. Thirty-four years after the introduction of the Act, the Prevention of Atrocities Act, 1989 was enacted with eighteen specified types of atrocities for penalty.

Colin Gonsalves, a Senior Advocate and the founder of the Human Rights Law Network, convincingly states, that "despite the existence of appropriate legal instruments to ensure the human rights of Dalits, the issue of an unequal access to State institutions, how the conventional village panchayati system has been a political and cultural form of oppression of Dalits. In these panchayats the Dalits have no right to present their cases or sit as equals with other dominant caste forces". Mr. Gonsalves further explains "that very few non-Dalit lawyers are ready to engage in cases on atrocities against Dalits. According to several Human Rights lawyers, there is a serious lack of special courts and special prosecutors. Almost all atrocities cases against Dalits go to regular sessions courts, which are already overburdened. Moreover, the responses of the administration to atrocities and other Dalit Human Rights violations have been poor. The access to justice is further denied through police atrocities. In the state of Punjab alone, in the past five years, more than twenty Dalits have been killed in police custody, and hundreds have been tortured by the police in illegal custody for petty crimes and because the victims belong to a poor class, the offender goes free. The judicial accountability and the access to justice have become absent in states like Bihar, Chhattisgarh and Punjab. In the recent midday meal case of the Supreme Court of India, a judgement on nutrition schemes, through one common meal a day in the school, was imposed on elementary schools in all states of India. The reaction from various states, for instance Karnataka, is that of resistance to mix high caste children with Dalit children."

11. Begging and Homelessness: The Law in India

Legal texts, whether these are domestic or international, are mainly texts without social contexts, unless empathy is added to them. Psychologists define empathy as the ability to identify somewhat with an object or a person. Looking at the Indian Legislation on Beggary, empathy is thoroughly missing. The issue of begging and homelessness must be regarded as an issue of Land and People, where Articles 1 to 15 of the International Covenant on Economic, Social and Cultural Rights must be regarded as fundamental principles while discussing the rights of homeless people, and everybody's inherent right to development. The Bombay Prevention of Begging Act, 1959, which has also been extended to the Union Territory of Delhi, has defined begging through exterior, visible criteria, such as soliciting or receiving alms, exposing or exhibiting with the object of obtaining or extorting alms, or having no visible means of subsistence. After arresting the visible poor, who is by the way called "beggar" throughout the Act, a confidential report is prepared by the probation officer of the Social Welfare Department. This report, which entails reasons for detention, is not necessarily shared with the beggar. The report is also referred to as the confidential report. This has resulted in the majority of detainees not being aware of the factual grounds under which they have been detained and put in a so-called certified institution for minimum two and maximum 10 years.

The Act provides for no interaction with or participation

of the beggar, as to tracing the reasons for begging. Confidentiality of the report indicates the distrust towards certain communities of our society, and the non-intention and disinterest of our policy makers and legislators to deal with the factors triggering poverty. The core aim of the Act is the prevention of begging. However, the methods for doing so are entirely based upon isolating beggars for a short period through a penalty, which is actually a purposeless detention. The Act is attentive towards the visible means and judging the same in a rapid fashion. The definition of Begging in the Act provides with no information on reasons for becoming a beggar, and no linkage to the anti- social forces leading to begging.

The Indian Constitution, through its directive principles, aims at a Welfare State. The objectives of a Welfare State is two-fold: it provides a wide range of benefits to be made available by the State to the citizens as of their right, but at the same time, it enhances the power of the bureaucracy, since the benefits thus provided are inevitably administered by government departments or their agents. The latter is surely maintained, but the responsibilities towards its citizens are forgotten. Because the aim of a Welfare State and jurisprudence is the social development of all citizens of India, rehabilitation and not punishment, should be looked at as a core aim while preventing begging. The Act is clearly unconstitutional from a welfare perspective. Moreover, the Constitution of India is a social document and the interpretation of its rights should be in the direction and with the aim of social equality, which this Act certainly has no residue of. Judgementalism prevails throughout the act, labelling people as beggars, and having no futuristic approach towards combating begging as a reason for poverty. By tracing reasons for begging, a rehabilitation process of the reasons and results of the problem of begging can be put in system in the already existing institutions. This would ensure social development, which for any human rights sensitive person, certainly is the core aim of law.

The regular claim made is that those who beg may not be what they seem—that they may, in fact, not be destitute but rather are part of an organized begging ring, fraudulently cashing in on public sympathy. Such a claim is both counterintuitive and factually incorrect. Begging tends to increase in times of social and economic downturn, which suggests that it is not a lifestyle choice, and the fact that the vast majority of the population choose not to beg demonstrates that there is probably little truth to the claim that it is an easy way to make a lot of money.

Labelling the Poor

The Labelling theory within psychology states that one of the factors that maintains and accelerates criminal conduct is the offender's sense of stigmatization, which takes form during the criminal justice processing. This produces negative effects on the person's sense of identity, and is likely to promote persistence in a criminal path/career.

Labelling is a fairly simple phenomenon, especially in social structures where economic and social disparities are many. This can be avoided through so-called diversion programmes, where young offenders are diverted from the justice system, and especially from institutionalization. This can be accomplished through alternative programmes such as mediation and reparation, or through social work intervention. It is of utmost significance to comprehend the term of labelling within psychology, and the effects on an individual or group of individuals, when the legislator or law enforcer applies labelling in their operations. Such operations easily result in segregation and class-oriented societies.

The social responsibilities of the Welfare State is a strong argument against the Act. Another is that the State is a guarantor of the rule of law, which in general terms requires that government be conducted in accordance with rules rather than on an arbitrary or highly discretionary basis. This allows citizens to exercise personal autonomy in planning their lives according to such rules, as well as ensuring that their rights and liberties are recognized and protected. Adherence to the rule of law is considered a hallmark of liberal democratic societies. The International Commission of Jurists states that the rule of law should seek to 'create and maintain the conditions which will uphold the dignity of man as an individual' through the recognition of civil, political rights and social rights. In order for this to be achieved, the laws imposed in a rule of law society must possess certain characteristics.

The law must be capable of being known, that is, it must have clarity and specificity. If this is not the case, citizens will not be able to exercise that autonomy which the rule of law is supposed to ensure. Blanket prohibitions against begging, such as those that exist in India, may be criticized for lacking clarity and specificity. Begging is seldom defined in legislation. Thus the distinction between begging and other forms of street level economic activity may be unclear. Another requirement of the rule of law is generality. That is, laws should have equal operation with respect to all citizens. It may be argued that this is a quality that prohibitions against begging do not possess. Anti-begging provisions effectively criminalize poverty and homelessness. Those who are able to meet their immediate needs will have no need to beg and will, therefore, not be liable for prosecution under such laws.

Further, laws that criminalize poverty and homelessness, such as begging offences, may be selectively enforced as a means of sweeping homeless people from the streets or encouraging them to move on. A "condemning criminal justice system" will only silence the human suffering, not cure it. The acknowledgement of the same is based on how the law is formulated, and how domestic courts do the interpretation. A high level of general, social, political, moral and legal education on the one hand, and a high standard of living on the other, are the two indispensable conditions for the achievement and implementation of the high ideals expressed in the two ideas of human rights and fundamental freedoms. It is true that a real observance of human rights is possible only in a true democracy as opposed to a "paper" democracy, which applies an "artificial rule of law". The criminalization of begging may be both unconstitutional and contrary to international human rights law.

While putting forth recommendations on alternatives to the current legislation, where a proper definition of rehabilitation should be given, we must include strong articles for our children on the streets, their rehabilitation where their right to growth and development, both mental and physical, is taken care of.

It is unfortunate but true, that this piece of legislation has no component of social engineering and justice towards a great number of people who were deprived of social equality at the time of their birth, the so-called beggars. While the rest of the conscious world is going in the direction of social jurisprudence, seemingly through such legislations, India is moving away from it. The Bombay Prevention of Begging Act, 1959, strongly fails the global principle of All Human Rights For All.

'60 per cent of those rescued from streets are mentally ill'

Bangalore: At the shelter for beggars and the homeless run by the government on the outskirts of the city, 60 per cent of those rescued from the streets have been found to be mentally ill, H. Sudarshan, Commissioner for Vigilance (Healthcare) of the Lokayukta has said. "There are so-called beggars' homes in Bangalore and Mysore, where people are detained under the Prevention of Beggary Act. But the mentally ill among them do not get psychiatric treatment and counselling they badly need," he said. Mr. Sudarshan donated cash received as an award and collected money from friends overseas to help the poor. "The Manasa project, which will now be implemented in Mysore, and later in Bangalore, will care for the mentally ill who have no place to go other than the streets. They need much more than food, clothing and shelter. Even hospitals cannot keep them beyond a few days at a time. Without proper psychiatric care, they can never fend for themselves," he said. The first Manasa community project will comprise a care centre, hospital and play areas. It will offer transit care and special education to the young. A helpline will also be launched. Mental health care will be provided in coordination with nearby primary health centres and doctors who volunteer to offer help.

"We want to bring out a positive change in the government's policy towards the mentally ill who are also homeless," Mr. Sudarshan said. Manasa will receive help from social activist and author Usha Shetty. She will donate for the cause proceeds from the sale of her book on caring for animals, *Le'mme Live My Life*. The organization, "For The Cause," will arrange publishing of books, and organize book festivals, art shows, musical events and sale of handmade and herbal products to raise funds, Ms. Shetty observed. "We are trying to make a beginning. There is need for more work among orphaned and homeless children who are just kept in shelters without any effort to integrate them with society once they are grown up," Mr. Sudarshan said. The homeless deserved a better deal from the more privileged, he noted.

Source: *The Hindu*, Wednesday, April 12, 2006

Police Violence and the Poor Child

A very common scene across the country's Juvenile Justice Boards (so-called Children's Courts), is a child's pledge not to be released from a so-called observation home, which is more or less a jail for children with some components of educational and vocational measures, because he fears police abuse and violence the moment he is released.

The Police Act of 1861 remains the central piece of legislation that governs all aspects of policing in India. The managerial feature of the police hierarchy was based on distrust of the lower ranks, an inheritance from the colonial rulers mainly to impose a regime police force upon their subjects which could be used solely to consolidate and perpetuate their rule in the country. This feature still prevails today. In fact, the 1861 Act instituted a police system designed to be absolutely subservient to the executive and highly authoritarian. As a result, in India, where more than 18 million children live and work on the streets, street children have been routinely detained illegally, beaten, and tortured and sometimes killed by police.

In 1995 and 1996, Human Rights Watch interviewed one

hundred street children; all reported a fear of the police, and sixty reported police abuse in the form of detentions, beatings, extortion, or verbal abuse. Fifteen-year-old Rakesh P., a porter in India, told HRW of being awoken by police on a railway platform and taken with three other boys to the police station. At the station, Rakesh P. was made to lie on his back with his arms outstretched. A policeman stood on each of his hands, and then his legs were tied and placed in the air. He said that this happened to all four boys. Another policeman started to beat their legs and feet with lathis, while the police called them thieves and sons of prostitutes. Rakesh P. said he was beaten for a long time and so badly that his legs and feet bled. The next morning the police sent the other children to observation homes, but they did not send Rakesh P. because they had injured him so badly they did not want a magistrate to see him. Instead, two strangers carried him to the street. He was not charged with any offence. Rakesh P. had to walk with a cane for eight weeks because of the injuries he sustained.

Furthermore, the oppressive and anti-child legislation is the Indian Prevention of Begging Act, which has forgotten the traumatic impact on children upon the sudden disappearance of their parents, or the support they found in the older person put behind bars on the basis of the Prevention of Begging Act. By temporary removing one generation of beggars and putting them behind bars (in so-called certified institutions), the legislator is creating a new generation of beggars. This situation demonstrates fixed perceptions about the homeless and destitute with legislators and policy-makers. For them, a homeless person, is more like an anti-social alien-like creature, with no responsibilities such as family or relations. This Act is another reason for the police to act harshly and release its frustrations on deprived communities.

Article 3 of the Convention on the Rights of the Child speaks of the "best interest of the child", assuming the State being the guarantor for the same, and not being a body offending the child, and applying corporal punishment and psychological repressions through oppressive legislations. Empathy through and in the form of sensitization is a must.

Case Law from Other Countries: Begging and the Right to Equality Before the Law

The right to equality before the law is recognized in Article 7 of the UDHR and Article 14 of the ICCPR. It may be argued that the creation of laws targeted at regulating the behaviour of homeless people, coupled with the selective enforcement of those laws, may amount to the infringement of homeless persons' right to equality before the law. Equality requires that those who are similarly situated should be treated the same, and those who are situated differently should be treated differently—difference should not lead to disadvantage. However, vagrancy laws, including anti-begging provisions, contravene the principle of equality by criminalizing the poor and homeless. Anti-begging provisions will have no effect with respect to those members of the community who do not need to engage in such behaviour for their survival. In her paper *Defending Begging Offenders*, Dr. Tamara Walsh compares and finds support in International Law to bring up the rights of beggars. Below are extracts from Dr. Walsh's paper.

The Fourteenth Amendment to the US Constitution protects citizens against laws which 'deny to any person. the equal protection of the laws'. In *Papachristou vs City of Jacksonville* the US Supreme Court criticized vagrancy laws on the basis that they make certain activities criminal that are 'normally innocent' by modern standards.[97] There was some suggestion in that case that this may contribute to their facial unconstitutionality under the Fourteenth Amendment. In *Blair vs Shanahan* the court found the distinction made in *Young* between begging by individuals and the solicitation for funds by charities to violate the Fourteenth Amendment because it did not treat alike all those who approach others and speak to them. In *Pottinger vs City of Miami* it was held that the selective enforcement of certain criminal laws against homeless people was impermissible since such people were engaging in life-[98] sustaining activities and had no private place to retreat to. Anti-begging offences treat like situations differently by drawing a distinction between those who beg and those who request other forms of assistance of strangers such as

97. 405 US 156 (1972) 162.
98. 810 F Supp 1551 (1992) 1578.

directions or the time, and by differentiating begging from other forms of informal street level activity, such as trick-or-treating or the sale of raffle tickets in public places. Thus, begging offences treat both differing circumstances alike and like behaviour differently resulting in inequality before the law. [99]

Begging Amounts to 'Speech' or 'Expression'

There was initially some debate in the US courts over whether begging constituted expressive conduct. In *Young vs New York City Transit Authority*, the majority of the US Court of Appeals of the Second Circuit held that begging was not inseparably intertwined with a particularized message because those who beg are not doing so to convey a message but rather to collect money.[100] This is despite the fact that a decade earlier in *Village of Schuamburg vs Citizens for a Better Environment et al.* the US Supreme Court held that solicitations by charities amounted to protected speech because their appeals were 'characteristically intertwined with informative and perhaps persuasive speech-seeking support for particular causes or for particular views on economic, political or social issues'.[101] The arguments of speech and communication had their basis in Article 19 of the *Universal Declaration of Human Rights* (UDHR) and Article 19(2) of the *International*

99. 'Defending Begging Offenders,' Tamara Walsh, QUT, *Law & Justice Journal,* Vol. 4, No. 1, 2004.
100.903 F 2d 146 (1990).
101.444 US 620 (1980) 632.

Covenant on Civil and Political Rights ICCPR) protect the right to freedom of expression. In both documents, the right is said to include the freedom to 'seek, receive and impart information and ideas' of all kinds. It therefore goes beyond the freedom of political communication which also exists under Indian domestic law, encompassing communication on all subjects, provided the rights and reputations of others, national security, public order, and public health and morals are protected.

In Canada, Section 2(b) of the *Canadian Charter of Rights and Freedoms* protects a general freedom of expression, which has been interpreted and applied in a manner very similar to its equivalent in the US. In *Federated Anti-Poverty Groups of British Columbia vs Vancouver (City)* the Supreme Court of British Columbia held that begging is indeed a form of speech protected under the Charter as it is 'a tool used by those in poverty to engage with the rest of society about their plight'. Consistent with the US approach, the court held that since the ordinance in question did not place a blanket prohibition on begging but rather was narrowly targeted at preventing certain kinds of begging behaviour and prohibited begging only in a narrowly defined set of circumstances (e.g. outside automatic teller machines and banks), it did not violate s 2(b) of the Charter.[102]

---

102. Scrutiny of Acts and Regulations Committee of Victoria, *Review of the Vagrancy Act 1966: Final Report* (Government Printer for the State of Victoria, 2002) 16; P. Lynch, 'Begging for Change: Homelessness and the Law' (2002) 26 *Melbourne University Law Review* 690, 694; M. Horn and M. Cooke, *A Question of Begging: A*

Important to note is that, in both the US and Canada, the courts have held that begging amounts to 'speech' or 'expression' in the relevant sense. Further, the courts in both countries have held that incursions on the right to freedom of expression will only be justified under certain circumstances. These exceptions have accorded closely with those listed in the relevant UDHR and ICCPR articles, such as public safety and the protection of the rights and freedoms of others.

Begging and the Right to Liberty

The right to liberty is recognized in Article 3 of the UDHR and Article 9 of the ICCPR. Liberty, or freedom of person, encompasses the capacity of individuals to pursue economic, social and cultural development through means of their own choosing. For its operational definition, it may again help to examine the US and Canadian case law. In *Federated Anti-Poverty Groups of British Columbia vs Vancouver City,* the court held that the ability to provide for one's self falls within the ambit of the right to liberty and thus anti-

---

Study of the Extent and Nature of Begging in the City of Melbourne (Hanover Welfare Services, 2001) 6, 7; H. Dean, 'Introduction' in H. Dean (ed) *Begging Questions: Street Level Economic Activity and Social Policy Failure* (Policy Press, 1999) 1. K. Driscoll and L. Wood, *A Public Life: Disadvantage and Homelessness in the Capital City* (RMIT Centre for Apllied Social Research, 1998) 4-5, 7; A. Schafer, *Down and Out in Winnipeg and Tornoto: The Ethics of Legislating Against Panhandling* (Caledon Institute of Social Policy, 1998) 3, 12; see also *Federated Anti-Poverty Groups of British Columbia vs Vancouver (City)* 2002 BCSC 105 [67].

begging laws may infringe this right.[103] The court's reasoning on this issue appears to be based on the fact that if one is not able to provide for one's self, all other rights lose their meaning. The court stated that: 'a person who lacks the basic means of subsistence ha[s] a tenuous hold on the most basic of constitutionally guaranteed human rights' and that 'without the ability to provide for those necessities, the entire ambit of other constitutionally protected rights becomes meaningless'. As noted above, since the ordinance in question in that case did not impose a blanket prohibition on begging, it was held not to result in a loss of liberty, the clear implication being that a blanket offence of begging, particularly one which provided for incarceration upon conviction, would amount to such a loss. Thus, anti-begging laws, which result in the imposition of penalties upon those who beg, may amount to an infringement of the right to liberty.[104]

In *Benefit vs Cambridge* Massachusetts' highest court held that to prohibit begging is to prohibit individuals from 'engaging with fellow human beings with the hope of receiving aid and compassion'.[105] Begging prohibitions tell those who are poor that they must suffer in silence. Moreover, they deprive members of the general public of interactions with their fellow human beings who are in

---

103. *Federated Anti-Poverty Groups of British Columbia vs Vancouver (City)* 2002 BCSC 105, [67].

104. Defending Begging Offenders, Tamara Walsh, QUT *Law & Justice Journal,* Vol. 4, No. 1, 2004.

105. 424 Mass 918 (1997).

difficulty. For some people, an encounter with a beggar might provoke them to action, result in self-enlightenment, create a social or empathic bond, and/or enable them to fulfil moral or religious obligations to assist those in need. Therefore, it might be argued in line with this reasoning that anti-begging laws violate certain aspects of the right to liberty.

Right to Freedom from Discrimination

Under Articles 2(1) and 26 of the ICCPR, Article 2(2) of the ICESCR and Article 2 of the UDHR, all persons are entitled to freedom from discrimination on the basis of race, colour, sex, language, religion, political or other opinion, national or social origin, property, birth or other status. The addition of 'or other status' implies that the principle of non-discrimination is intended to be flexible enough to extend to other bases of discrimination which remain uncontemplated by the provisions. It is proposed that one such status, which should be recognized as a legitimate ground of discrimination is socio-economic status, and that begging offenders may be defended on this basis. The impermissibility of punishing status has been recognized in both the US and Canada, and there has been litigation in both jurisdictions on the subject of whether socio-economic status, homelessness or poverty may properly be characterized as a 'status'. In *Powell v Texas,* the US Supreme Court held that when determining whether status was being punished by a law, the focus should be on whether the act punished was volitional and thus whether the defendant was able to avoid it as a matter of fact. Similarly, in *Federated Anti-Poverty Groups of British Columbia vs Vancouver (City)* the Supreme Court of British Columbia held that in order for a certain 'status' to constitute a ground of discrimination under Section15 (1) of the Charter, it must be established that the relevant characteristic cannot be changed.

12. The Girl Child and Woman in India

"She has the right to participate in the minute details of the activities of man and she is entitled to a supreme place in her own sphere of activity as man is in his."[106]

- Mahtma Gandhi

India occupies a strategic position in Asia, being the largest of the South Asian countries, with a population of over one billion. Women constitute a population of 495.74 million, with 360.52 million in rural and 135.22 million in urban areas. The human development status of women shows wide interstate and intrastate variations. India's human development is marked by a paradox that has seen a systematic decline in women's status despite recent advances in women's education and economic status. It is indeed puzzling that the economic development of women has not brought a commensurate change in their social development.[107]

India became a signatory to the Convention on the Elimination of All Forms of Discrimination against Women (CEDAW) in 1980 and ratified it in 1993. India submitted a declaration regarding Articles 5(a) and 16(1) that reiterates India's commitment to abiding by the

---

106.M.K. Gandhi, *Women and Social Injustice*, Navjeevan Publishing House, Ahmedabad, p.4 (1947).

107.Prasad, Kiran, "Preface". In Kiran Prasad (ed). *Communication and Empowerment of Women: Strategies and Policy Insights from India*. New Delhi: The Women's Press (2004).

provisions "in conformity with its policy of non-interference in the personal affairs of any community without its initiative and consent." India also registered a declaration regarding Article 16(2) on minimum marriage ages and compulsory registration; although India fully supports the principle, "it is not practical in a vast country like India with its variety of customs, religions and level of literacy."

India acceded to the Convention on the Rights of the Child (CrC) in 1992, with a declaration regarding the progressive implementation of Article 32 thereof on child labour, particularly with reference to paragraph 2(a) on the provision of a minimum employment age.

India declared 2001 as Women's Empowerment Year for the country, and the National Policy for Empowerment of Women of India was released the same year. Women's empowerment depends, to a large extent, on the degree of access to and control of women over different means of communication or mass media. The oppressed and marginalized groups, including women, are often excluded in coverage by communication channels. Communication for women's empowerment is a participatory process wherein women activists and groups have begun to break away from their state of powerlessness to question the status quo that oppresses them when negative social values and cultural norms are disseminated through different media. India's National Policy for Empowerment of Women, an official policy document of the Government of India, includes measures to promote societal awareness to gender issues and human rights, and the use of different forms of mass media to communicate social messages related to women's equality and empowerment.

Women in India continue to labour under the brunt of oppressive traditions, exploitation, and lack of self-worth or identity. This essay is an effort to underline the current collision between strong women's rights expressions prevailing in India and a static view on law and legislation.

Indian History and Women

There is a widespread view among scholars that the best way to judge a nation's progress is to find out how it looks at the status of women. Indeed, many researchers have equated cultural levels with the types of treatment meted out to women and have found that there is a strong correlation between law and status of women and the cultural levels of a society.[108]

Many have traced the enunciation of a liberal social attitude vis-à-vis women to the pristine sources of Hindu Vedic philosophy.[109] The late 19th century's research noted the high status of women in the Vedic period, when they

108.D.N. Majumdar, *Races and Cultures of India*, Asia Publishing House, Bombay, p.251 (1989).

109.The Vedic civilization is the Indo-Aryan culture associated with the Vedas, the earliest known records of Indian history. Mainstream scholarship places the Vedic civilization into the 2nd and 1st millennia participated fully in religious rituals, had freedom of movement, were educated, married fairly late, and had a right to decide whom to marry. Widow remarriage was permitted and unmarried or married women also enjoyed an honoured position in family and society.[110] A woman in the Vedic age was the husband's companion in weal and woe, an equal partner in all activities.

Degradation in the position of women, however, was a fact when famous jurists like Manu remarked:[111]

"Women in her childhood must remain under the custody of her father, in youth she must remain under the custody of her husband and when widowed she must remain under the custody of her sons. She must never be independent. Women whether minor or young or old, must not act

BC, while some Hindu scholars date its beginnings as early as the 5th millennium BC based on alleged astronomical information in the Vedas.

110. A.S. Altekar, *The Position of Women in Hindu Civilization*, Motilal Banarasi Dass Publishers, Delhi, p.235 (1959).

111. The *Manu Smriti* translated "Laws of Manu" or "Institutions of Manu", is a foundational work of Hindu law and ancient Indian society, written c.200 in India. It is one of the eighteen Smritis of the Dharma Sastra (or "laws of righteous conduct"); smriti means "what is remembered" and is applied to a Hindu text other than the Vedas, including traditional Indian epics, the Puranas, and science and grammar treatises. Unlike the Vedas which are considered of divine origin, the Smritis are considered to be of human origin. They contain laws, rules and codes of conduct to be applied by individuals, communities and nations. Some of these laws codify the Hindu caste system and discuss the "stages of life for a twice-born man".

independently in the house. It is a sin for women to offer sacrifice or fast. Her duty is only to serve her husband and in case of his death she must never think of a second husband. She must eat less to pass the rest of her life. To tell lies is the nature of women".[112]

Manu continues:

"The truth, however, is that the male is the enjoyer and female a thing to be enjoyed". The bride is given to the bridegroom with a solemn declaration "Like a dining leaf (which cannot be used by another person), she is unfit to be enjoyed by another person".[113]

It is evident from Sanskrit works that women were jealously and strictly guarded, and in no state of life were they independent. However, at the same time there was no want of the feeling that it is the moral and not the physical means, which serve as a safeguard against temptation.

During the golden periods of Indian history under the Mauryas[114] and the Guptas[115], there was a gradual erosion of women's rights. Regressive customs like child marriage, *purdah* (veil), and *sati* (bride burning ritual) began in the turbulent times that followed.[116] The position of common

112.*Manu Smiriti*, Chapter V, Sloka; 147-157.

113.Ibid.

114.The Mauryan Empire lasted from 321 to 185 BCE.

115.The Gupta Empire lasted from 320 to 550.

116.Verma and Verma, *Indian Women through the Ages*, Great India Publishers, New Delhi, p.11 (1976).

women did not improve during the Muslim time. At the time of the advent of the British rule, the position of women in India was at its lowest ebb. Child marriage was in vogue. Sati was prevalent. Female literacy was considered a source of moral danger. Dancing girls had lucrative professions.[117]

By the end of 19th century, there had emerged many leaders of the women's movements. In the 1920s and 1930s women participated in the non-cooperation and civil disobedience movements against the British in India, and many served jail sentences. The All India Women's Conference became the major vehicle for the women's movement, shifting from welfare requests to demands of full political and legal equality in all areas. When India finally became independent, the Congress Government implemented many demands of the All India Women's Conference, which included legislation for prohibiting polygamy, liberalizing divorce, and granting equal inheritance rights to women.[118]

Mahatma Gandhi placed the question of women's emancipation in its proper perspective, as an integral part of a larger process of social transformation. For Mahatma Gandhi freedom of the nation was the sum total of the freedom of all individuals.[119]

---

117. Azim Sherwani, *The Girl Child in Crisis*, Indian Social Institute, New Delhi, p.13 (1998).
118. Ibid.
119. M.K. Gandhi, *Constructive Programme* quoted in the UN, *Harijan*, March 25 (1939).

The Girl Child and the Law

The inherent right of the child to life is a fundamental principle in International Child Rights as well as in Human Rights in general. What differentiates the child's right to life from the general Human Right to life is that the child's right goes beyond a mere right to not have its life taken. The child's right-to-life includes the fact that a child is by its very definition an evolving and growing person. Therefore, in order to ensure and guarantee a child's normal growth and development it is only natural that constant consideration for a child's mental health should be included in laws and enactments where child rights are discussed. This means that the child also has a right to grow and develop. The UN Convention on the Rights of the Child, 1989 states that "State Parties shall ensure to the maximum extent possible the survival and development of the child." Article 25 states: "State Parties recognize the right of a child who has been placed by the competent authorities for the purpose of care, protection or treatment of his or her physical or mental health, to a periodic review of the treatment and all other circumstances relevant to his or her placement."

With regard to the victim and the application of psychological considerations and support, the criticism indicates how the application of capital punishment is viewed to be the settler of justice for victims. However, applying this punishment and completely disregarding rehabilitation and social assistance as recommended in the Declaration of Basic Principles of Justice for Victims of Crime and Abuse of Power, adopted by General Assembly resolution 40/34 of November 29, 1985, cannot be a matter of a justice system which should balance the rights of the victims with the rights of the offenders. What is important to note here is the definition of "victims" and their "assistance" put forth under Section *A. Victims of Crime:* (selected provisions)

> 1."Victims" means persons who, individually or collectively, have suffered harm, including physical or mental injury, emotional suffering, economic loss or substantial impairment of their fundamental rights, through acts or omissions that are in violation of criminal laws operative within Member States, including those laws proscribing criminal abuse of power.
>
> 2. A person may be considered a victim, under this Declaration, regardless of whether the perpetrator is identified, apprehended, prosecuted or convicted and regardless of the familial relationship between the perpetrator and the victim. The term "victim" also includes, where appropriate, the immediate family or dependants of the direct victim and persons who have suffered harm in

intervening to assist victims in distress or to prevent victimization.

3. The provisions contained herein shall be applicable to all, without distinction of any kind, such as race, colour, sex, age, language, religion, nationality, political or other opinion, cultural beliefs or practices, property, birth or family status, ethnic or social origin, and disability.

Furthermore, with guidance from the restorative theory, the Declaration has elaborated on particular assistance factors, which are mentioned below.

4. Victims should receive the necessary material, medical, psychological and social assistance through governmental, voluntary, community-based and indigenous means.

5. Victims should be informed of the availability of health and social services and other relevant assistance and be readily afforded access to them.

6. Police, justice, health, social service and other personnel concerned should receive training to sensitize them to the needs of

victims, and guidelines to ensure proper and prompt aid.

7. In providing services and assistance to victims, attention should be given to those who have special needs because of the nature of the harm inflicted or because of factors such as those mentioned in paragraph 3 above.

Child Victims: Lack of Mental Health Considerations

Different Indian laws define a child variously. This variety in defining a child demonstrates the unpreparedness of the Indian legislator to deal with the added responsibility the moment a law is formed for a child. This unpreparedness has turned into a dreadful insensitivity—with a trauma not dealt with, and affecting generations. From a larger perspective, all of us should fear the devastating after-effects of sexual abuse, and other crimes against children behind closed doors.

Social scientists are now coming to believe that sexual abuse of children in India is far more prevalent than most people realize. The enormity of the problem can be realized by the fact that in India alone, at least 25 per cent of the adult population has been molested before the age of 16. At least 27 million females are adult survivors of child sexual abuse. Incest is the most common form of child abuse. Furthermore, the report by the Department of Women and

Child Development on the implementation of the Convention of Child Rights in India, prepared for the United Nations Committee on the Rights of the Child, has identified child sexual abuse as a priority issue for immediate action. What is crucial to note is the survey conducted by Sakshi, an NGO working for women's rights extensively, from 1996, where out of 109 judges, 50 per cent felt child sexual abuse is not common, and this "uncommon offence existed only amongst uneducated, depressed, and over-sexed people or people with a prostrate gland problem". Furthermore, these judges felt that abuses were mostly carried out by servants and least commonly within families.

Despite the gravity of the problem, the various facets of child abuse are never discussed within the educational system. The aforesaid becomes even more questionable, when our society and its various institutions constantly lecture its citizens on rights and wrongs, moral and ethics. Strangely, the educational system has missed out on informing its children that the moment an abuse has taken place –something *wrong* has taken place. This is nothing foreign at all—most civilized nations use the educational system as a crucial means to inform its children about *what amounts to a crime against a minor, and about the various victim support systems.* Maybe it is immature to believe that sensitive issues such as incest would be dealt with in a set-up which does not even believe in sex education in schools. There is a lack of a system of awareness, when the adult's accountability towards a child fails.

The laws dealing with sexual offences do not specifically address child sexual abuse. It is disconcerting but true, that the India Penal Code 1860 does not recognize child abuse. Only rape and sodomy can lead to criminal conviction. Anything "less than rape", as defined by the law, amounts to 'outraging the modesty'. These laws are problematic when applied to adult women, but they are even more difficult when applied to children. While Section 376 of the IPC seeks to provide women redress against rape, it is rarely interpreted to cover the broad range of sexual abuses particularly of children that actually takes place. The word 'rape' is too specific, this does not include abuse on 'boys'; moreover, 'intercourse' is often interpreted to mean with an 'adult'.

In *Sakshi vs Union of India*, the Supreme Court of India asked the Law Commission to consider certain important issues regarding sexual abuse of children submitted by the petitioner and the feasibility of amendment to Sections 375 and 376 IPC.[120] Hopefully, the forthcoming amendment will also deal with aftermath issues of child sexual abuse. The abused children commonly suffer from serious mental and physical effects, either immediately or later in life, from emotional and behavioural problems to abnormal sexual behaviour and psychiatric disorders. Suicidal tendencies and drug abuse are common long-term effects as well. Child-related concepts are gravely missing in the Indian laws. A victim of crime, and more so if the victim is a child undergoing trauma, needs to be treated with care.

120.Case no: (1999) 8 SCC 591.

The facilities with regard to emergency reception of victims of crime is lacking to a great extent. There are no mental health professionals to deal with the trauma-stricken victims. Moreover, the victims who do not have signs of serious physical injury are released immediately without any psychiatric treatment.

Furthermore, in *Majlis Manch vs State of Maharashtra & Ors.* A 9-year-old deaf and mute girl institutionalized in an observation home, was raped and the medical examination indicated, "Skin injury mark. Bite mark on right cheek and multiple abrasion marks over skin, buttocks and both legs". Even in such a dreadful case, where the child is not able to express pain or explain even minimally what has happened to her, even in such cases there has been no realization or will to make mental health considerations an inextricable component of law. [121]

The medical examination mentioned the possibility of violent sexual assault, and the teeth bite marks were of the adult sexual assailant. By the interim order the Court directed the removal of the victim girl from the Observation Home to the Bal Asha Trust. The girl was in a serious condition and required medical aid and good nutrition, therefore the court directed the state government to deposit a sum of Rs. 50,000 with the Bal Asha Trust. When the girl was shifted to Bal Asha Trust she bit the other children, fought and expressed aggression, cowered under her bed when not having hysterics, displayed sexualized behaviour,

121. Criminal Writ Petition No.585 of 2000-Bombay High Court.

wept, would not allow herself to be touched, and was difficult when she was to be undressed for a bath.[122] Pinki Virani in her book *Bitter Chocolate*, explains "this child is a child again" a couple of months later when it appears that the girl is not mute, though mentally slow but not mute, and how "the power of true love in the form of real care" has brought about this transformation.[123]

Virani's conclusion is beyond due proportions, given the dreadful experiences of this particular girl child and her behaviour with other children. Merely the ability to talk again must not be seen as the sole demarcation of regaining all the lost aspects of health and self-esteem. What is crucial to ask here is whether the child has been guaranteed development as her rights as a child guarantees her? Has the violence around and inside her been removed for good? Has social justice as implied in Article 3 of the Convention on the Rights of the Child, which strongly suggests interdisciplinary, i.e. socio-legal and psycho-legal methodologies been taken care of? In all actions concerning children, whether undertaken by public or private social welfare institutions, courts of law, administrative authorities or legislative bodies, the best interests of the child shall be a primary consideration. Has Justice Suba Rao's statement "Social Justice must begin with the child; unless a tender plant is properly nourished, it has little chance of growing into a strong and useful tree. So, first priority in the scalc of social justice should be given to the welfare of children,"

122. Pinki Virani, *Bitter Chocolate,* Penguin Books India (2000), p. 85.
123. Ibid.

been taken care of in this particular case.[124] Has "competent supervision" been granted to the child, according to the aforesaid article?

Mental Health Experts on Majlis Manch vs State of Maharashtra & Ors.

Col. Goel, National Consultant (Mental Health), Directorate General of Health Services, Ministry of Health & Family Welfare, Government of India, further adds to *Majlis Manch vs State of Maharashtra & Ors.*, that the girl will also require mental health interventions at several levels and on a continuing basis to deal with the severe psychological trauma resulting from the rape. Col. Goel adds: "Mental health issues related to children/ adolescents need to be conceptualized differently from those involving adults. Children are not miniaturized adults. Their perceptions/responses to traumatic events or other severe stressors are qualitatively different and the therapeutic interventions required are much more complex, requiring specialized skills. The present legal system in India is completely blind to these issues and the first step should be to initiate sensitization programmes for serving police/judicial officers and to introduce the requisite changes in the training curricula in police/judicial training academies and law schools. The legal framework, including the Indian Penal Code as well as the Criminal Procedure Code, also needs to

124. Suba Rao, *Social Justice and Law* (1974), p. 110.

be restructured... Our knowledge relating to crucial child/adolescent mental health issues, like ADHD, dyslexia, delinquency, is even more inexact/ controversial than that involving adults and the long-term implication of court decisions in such matters can be extremely serious/far-reaching".[125]

Professor Malavika Kapur, of the National Institute of Advanced Studies, Indian Institute of Science, Bangalore, explains that the case may have been of an intellectually disabled child who has been sexually abused, a fairly common practice in Indian orphanages.[126] The issue of her intellectual disabilty has seemingly been overlooked in the judicial process. The Indian legal system has tended to neglect the needs of children and is often ruled by the adult considerations in the cases of abuse (physical, emotional or sexual), of child custody or child labour. Prof. Kapur elaborates: "In one of the ancient Ayurvedic paediatric textbooks called *Kashyapa Samhita* on child care it is stated that a children's physician should be a great scholar and an experienced practioner who should not commit any errors of judgement in the treatment of children. If he does, as a consequence he will suffer great burden of guilt all his life."

125.Col. Goel, is the National Consultant (Mental Health), Directorate General of Health Services, Ministry of Health & Family Welfare, Government of India. The interview with Col. Goel took place on September 3, 2005.

126.Professor Malavika Kapur, of National Institute of Advanced Studies, Indian Institute of Science, Bangalore. The interview with Prof. Kapur took place in August 2005.

She further states that "lawyers too should have a similar code of conduct. Children's concerns are too serious to be handled by novices. The stakes though not high materially, are very high in terms of ethics and the present and the future psycho-social development of children. Indian legal experts should be especially sensitized to mental health needs of the children and the promotion of psycho-social development of children".

Dr. Mathiharan, an expert of Forensic Medicine with the Institute of Legal Medicine in Chennai, Tamil Nadu, after reading an abstract from *Majlis Manch vs State of Maharashtra & Ors.*, underlines that an obstetrician should have examined the victim when she was brought to the hospital after the offence and medical practitioners should properly document the examination. The victims of sexual offences may not suffer from physical injuries. Dr. Mathiharan elaborates that the psychological trauma will be more acute and they require immediate and long-term psychiatric assistance.[127]

Ms. Ratna Golaknath, a Mental Health Therapist from Saarthak, New Delhi, underlines that the first approach has to be a child rights approach of protecting the rights of the child to development. In this case the developmental

127.Dr. K. Mathiharan is an expert of Forensic Medicine with the Institute of Legal Medicine in Chennai, Tamil Nadu, an institute, which has focus areas such as Medical Law, Medical Ethics, Forensic Medicine, Consumer Rights, and Human Rights. The interview took place on June 16, 2005.

needs require special attention. It is also extremely important to help the child access support from professionals who can address the trauma and impact of the sexual abuse and work with the child towards a rediscovery of self and outgrowing the pain. Speaking from an Indian perspective, Ms. Golaknath explains that, at present, we do not have homes that are inclusive and well-trained to accommodate the child. It would be necessary for the court or the law to develop a care plan for the child, which includes the input from professionals in various fields. Special educators, counsellors, care providers are needed. She elaborates by stating that it is important also for advocates to lobby for the development of mandatory care plans for each child. The court should be able to ask an NGO for a follow up and should make a requirement for each child to be given a similar individualized plan. It is the child's right as well as the child's need to be treated with dignity, respect and as an individual with access to resources for development.[128]

Ms. Arvinder J. Singh, is a therapist and has worked extensively with child victims in Jammu and Kashmir.[129] She furthers speaks on the *Majlis Manch* case by stating that one must defocus from the word rape and refocus on

128. Ms. Ratna Golaknath is a Mental Health Therapist at Saarthak, an organization which works extensively on the Right to Mental Health. It is based in New Delhi and is headed by Dr. Achal Bhagat. The interview with Ms. Golaknath took place on September 3, 2005.

129. The interview with Ms. Arvinder J. Singh took place on July 7, 2005 in New Delhi.

its psychological effects. Good nutrition in this particular case is probably not as important as a caring physical touch, so that trust can be regained. Ms. Singh, in this context, recalls a case from Kashmir, where she was training a group of children out of whom one lame girl would sit in a dark corner the whole day. This girl had been gang-raped and her brother was killed. The girl could not understand Hindustani; she spoke Kashmiri, and could therefore not talk to Ms. Singh during the sessions. Ms. Singh decided to reach out to her and touch the girl and to give her a warm eye contact, which made the girl break down and cry while embracing Ms. Singh. "Sometimes it is not about deafness or muteness, it is what environment you are providing the child, the very presence is what a child understands, not necessarily the words", Ms. Singh explains.

Dr. Bhargavi Davar, of the Centre for Advocacy in Mental Health, Pune, adds that the girl experiences multiple levels of vulnerability, namely, girl child, girl child with multiple disabilities, and girl child within an institution.[130] Her needs then are multiple and need to be assessed with these levels of vulnerabilities in mind. It is surprising that 'good nutrition' is suggested as part of rehabilitation for rape. Dr. Davar explains that the girl needs a child-sensitive person to work with her in the long term on her experience of the rape. Being a child, and being exposed to such a high level of trauma, her needs will go beyond verbal

130.The interview with Dr. Davar took place on November 25, 2005.

expression. She may be afraid of touch, men, etc. These will have to be addressed sensitively and using also non-verbal healing techniques. Perhaps a community service programme will be able to organize foster care for her, or maybe she can be sent back to her family. The legal context or her social situation is not very clear. In any case, she will require psycho-social care in the long term. Most important to understand is, wherever she is, this will have to be continued. Many mental health professionals treat symptoms with drugs. She would probably end up receiving tranquillizers or anti-depressant medication for any symptoms she may experience. The social context cannot be medicalized. Such treatments (giving pills for social problems) converts structural barriers and crimes into simplistic relief measures, and lets the perpetrators, such as the rapist here, go scotfree.

Most psychiatrists in India do not recognize violence against women as a structural issue. Restoration of a justice environment is an important mental health strategy in contexts where a social problem caused the trauma, such as this one. This would be the first step to take, for the girl to feel a sense of security and sanity, Dr. Davar concludes.

Furthermore, in India, the duty of the medical professional is to examine the child victim and gather information that will protect and/or validate the traumatized child. In the cases of refusal to undergo a medical examination the child is referred to a therapist, but only for issues that are making the child uncooperative.[131] Important to note and compare is how the American School Counsellors Association (ASCA) published a position statement on child abuse in 1988, defining the act as "the infliction by other than accidental means of physical harm upon the body of a child, continual psychological damage or denial of emotional needs". Examples of child abuse given in the statement include extensive or patterned bruises, burns, lacerations, welts, or abrasions; injuries inconsistent with explanation; sexual abuse, molestation, or exploitation; emotional disturbances caused by friction or discord in the home or mentally ill parents; and cruel treatment. However, most significant is that ASCA defined child neglect as "the failure to provide necessary food, care, clothing, shelter, supervision, or medical attention for a child", and described this behaviour as lack of supervision or medical attention, irregular and illegal school absences; over-working or exploiting the child; lack of nurturance; or abandonment.[132]

It is appalling to find the debate surrounding legislation on children and their mental health virtually absent, and opinions of legal experts almost non-existent. Aspects such as psychological assistance and mental health concerns as a means to regain the 'lost innocence' of a child, and how such rehabilitation can break the cycle of violence, have

131. Marukh Adenwalla, *Child Sexual Abuse and the Law*, India Centre for Human Rights and Law (2000), p.85.

132. Charles L. Thompson, Linda B. Rudolph, *Counselling Children*, 3rd ed., Brooks/Cole Publishing Company Pacific Grove, California, (1992), p.354.

been missed out in the lawmakers' priorities or in the training of lawyers and judges.

Secondary Victimization of the Child: The Lack of Preventive Features in Law

Research and professional experience shows that secondary victimization, generated either by institutions or individuals, is often experienced by victims in the aftermath of crime and leaves them in need of help. Secondary victimization involves a lack of understanding of the suffering of victims which can leave them feeling both isolated and insecure, losing faith in the help available from their communities and professional agencies.[133] The experience of secondary victimization intensifies the immediate consequences of crime by prolonging or aggravating the victim's trauma; attitudes, behaviour, acts or omissions can leave victims feeling alienated from society as a whole.

According to Dr. Preethi, no child is safe; every child is vulnerable to sexual abuse. In her documentary *The Children We Sacrifice*, filmmaker Grace Poore calls sexually abused children the victims of a culture that prioritizes family harmony, honour and duty more than individual trauma and pain.[134] The "silence about sex" culture forbids

133. R.J. Lifton, 'Victims and Survivors', in B. Giamo and J. Grunberg (eds.), *Beyond Homelessness: Frames of Reference*, Iowa City, IA: University of Iowa Press (1992).

134. Rhonda Smith, 'Shedding Light on Taboo Topics,' *Washington Blade,* Friday, September 16, 2005.

parents from talking to their children about sexuality, and frowns upon any non-sexual intimate relationship with the opposite gender. The problem, according to the Chennai-based psychiatrist Dr. S. Vijayakumar, does not appear to be big simply because it is suppressed. These factors contribute to a high rate of child sexual abuse in India. Most often, sexually-abused children make no noise about their traumatic experiences. It is this that encourages offenders. Dr. Preethi convincingly states, that "this secrecy has to be broken"; for this, she lays stress on talking to children about sexual abuse, listening to them, believing them, and recognizing symptoms such as physical complaints and behavioural and psychological changes. She elaborates: "Silence does not mean all is fine with the child." A child's silence can be eloquent. [135]

According to a Voluntary Health Association India (VHAI) report, a child victim suffers four times—at the time of the offence, when narrating the incident, during medical examination and if brought to the court. According to the study, the silence about sex-related matters and the lengthy and cumbersome legal procedures perpetuate the problem in India. The average time taken for a sexual abuse case to find its way from the lower courts to the higher courts is 10-15 years. Between 1992 and 1994, 48 cases of child sexual abuse were reported in the newspapers. The children affected were in the 8-10 age group, barring one who was six months old. The VHAI report argues that if and when

135. Asha Krishnakumar, *Frontline*, 'Silent Victims,' Volume 20 - Issue 21, October 11 - 24, 2003.

the cases come to the court for hearing, the children would have become adults and may want to erase the nightmare of their experiences from their consciousness. Dragging the children and their mothers to court for years, is by definition and experience, a matter of severe secondary victimization, and is often worse than the offence itself.[136]

Lois J. Engelbrecht, a researcher working on the problems of child sexual abuse, quotes studies showing that over 50 per cent of children in India are sexually abused, a rate that is higher than in any other country. The physical fallout of abuse includes pregnancy at a young age, and incidence of HIV and other STDs. Equally devastating are the cognitive and emotional impact. Engelbrecht states, "Children are sometimes led to believe sex is love which lead some to behave very sexually. Often they become afraid of sex and make themselves ugly to avoid it. There is also a pervasive sense of powerlessness. Victims tend to think, 'I am now dirty; it's my fault.' There is also a high correlation between drug, alcohol and sexual abuse."[137] Huma Khan of the Kanpur-based Centre for the Study of Human Rights terms child sexual abuse as one of the least documented violations. Studies made across India, documented in Grace Poore's resource book *The Children We Sacrifice*, which accompany the documentary on sexually abused girls, show the wide prevalence of the problem.

---

136. Worldwide web: www.vhai.org, see "resource center"
137. *The Hindu Business Line*, Paromita Pain, Alert and Safe, Friday, January 7, 2005.

The Proposed Indian Commission for the Protection of Child Rights Bill, 2005: Going in Circles

> Naturally kids' courts matters aren't as serious as other matters. I think representing children is very good grounding for a new lawyer. You are not playing for terribly high stakes…also the complexity of matters …is not as serious.[138]

The Commission proposes to be the legal mechanism to oversee and review the implementation of the National Policy for Children. It will also help improve the survival rate, health, nutrition and education of children, particularly girls, and equip them to become economically productive adults. According to Chapter II of the Commissions of Protection of Child Rights Bill 2005, as introduced in the Lok Sabha, the proposed constitution suggests the inherent difficulty in determining the needs of a child who has come out of a traumatic experience, more or less.[139] Chapter II Section 3 (2) put forth the profile of the Commission's members as follows, a Chairperson who is a person of eminence and has done outstanding work for the promotion of children; and six members, one each from the following fields, to be appointed by the Central Government from amongst persons of eminence, ability, integrity, standing and

---

138. Edited by, Philip Alston, Stephen Parker, John Seymour, *Children, Rights, and the Law*, Clarendon Press, Oxford (1992), p.87.

139. The Lok Sabha (House of the People) is the lower house of India. Members of the Lok Sabha are directly elected by the electorate consisting of all the adult citizens of India.

experience, in education; child health, care, welfare, ***or*** child welfare; juvenile justice ***or*** care of neglected ***or*** marginalized children ***or*** children with disabilities; elimination of child labour ***or*** children in distress, child psychology ***or*** sociology; and laws relating to children

This particular chapter abruptly demonstrates the generalization of the special needs of the individual child. By mixing special needs of, for instance, child health and child welfare as interchangeable areas, or child psychology and sociology as filling the same functions in all situations for all children, the legislator and policy-maker have again indicated the inability to understand the importance of specialized representation in the form of experts as sociologists, ***and*** psychologists, ***and*** experts in child health ***and*** child welfare.

Chapter V of the proposed Bill, Section 25 and 26 regulates the constitution and functions of the Children's Courts. Section 25 states that for the purpose of providing speedy trial of offences against children or of violation of child rights, the state government may, with the concurrence of the Chief Justice of the High Court, by notification, specify at least a court in the State or specify, for each district, a Court of Session, to be a Children's Court. Furthermore, Section 26 states that for every Children's Court a Special Public Prosecutor should be appointed, or an advocate who has been in practice not less than seven years.[140]

140. Parul Sharma, 'Critical Case: Child Rights Bill,' *Tehelka the People's Paper*, September 17, 2005.

In *Vishal Jeet vs Union of India*, the Supreme Court directed steps be taken against child prostitution.[141] One directive was on establishing advisory committees with experts from all fields to make suggestions regarding measures for a number of matters including eradicating child prostitution, care and rehabilitation of rescued girls and setting up of rehabilitation homes. The judgement did indicate a good understanding of the sensitive situation of children coming out of prostitution. However, again the judiciary failed to understand the importance of defining 'rehabilitation' in its judgement. Experts may argue that defining such terminology is not within the mandate of the court. However, when directions concerning child rights are formulated it must be understood by law that either the inclusion of expert opinions is put in or that judges are sensitized towards issues such as child psychology. This should also be made applicable to the Juvenile Court, where a permanent position of a psychologist/mental health professional, is created alongside the judge to identify and precisely define directions on rehabilitation.

The vague mandate of the planned Children's Court is a repeat of the vague mandate expressed in the Indian Protection of Human Rights Act, 1993, where Human Rights Law could be anything under the sky. Again, a general sessions court will act as a guarantor for the implementation of rights; whether it is Human Rights or

141. AIR 1990 SC 1412.

Child Rights. Another unfortunate fact is the weight put on and importance given to the prosecution side where the appointment of a special prosecutor has been declared, but no appointment with regard to the growing and developing child has been taken care of. For instance, the expertise of child psychology within the court of law.

In my interview with Justice Sharma from the Rajasthan Higher Judicial Service, he initiated the interview by stating a "child is always innocent, one doesn't have to do understand much about them, they are like [a] blank paper". [142] Upon my asking how prepared a judge is to understand the sensitivity of a child, Justice Sharma responded by stating that the case-history explains the sensitivity of a child. When I took child labour as an example, and the trauma and mental state of a rescued child, asking Justice Sharma how a judge should approach such a child, he states that it must be understood that such a child is abnormal. It has to be explained by the judge, preferably the Principal Magistrate in the Juvenile Justice Board, as to what is normal. The judge has to explain who is a "good child" and who is a "bad child". It is important to understand, according to Justice Sharma, that it is the parents' fault that the child is a bonded labourer. "They are lacking consciousness, for instance in villages people are very cunning". Justice Sharma elaborates by explaining that child sensitivity has to be handled firmly. "If a child's

---

142. The interview took place on August 6, 2005 at Justice M.K. Sharma's residence in Jaipur.

grandfather beats him/her it is not reason enough not to go back home". He further elaborates that the Arya Samaj Home in Ajmer is the ideal set up for children who have been rescued from bonded labour or child delinquents.[143] Justice Sharma explains that children, whether neglected or young offenders, stay together in this home, and live a disciplined and controlled life, where they wake up early and chant Hindu *mantras.* These children are happy children when they are in a group, which indulge in highly cultural activities, according to Justice Sharma. I asked about the 'individual needs' of a child, and the importance paid to the same. The answer to my question was "children are children, all are the same". Upon my question whether Justice Sharma too belonged to the Arya Samaj, he confirmed that he did.

In my interview with Justice Parihar, Jaipur High Court, he explained that "there is no special law in India for the protection of children, but the notion of childhood is taken into consideration by a judge". Justice Parihar further stated *that even if* special consideration is given to children, "they will go back and be the same".[144] Justice Parihar

143. Arya Samaj (*Aryan Society* or *Society of Nobles*) is a Hindu reform movement in India that was founded by Swami Dayananda in 1875. He was a sannyasin (renouncer) who believed in the infallible authority of the Vedas. Dayananda advocated the doctrine of karma and reincarnation, and emphasized the ideals of *brahmacharya* (chastity) and *sanyasa* (renunciation).

144. The interview took place on August 6, 2005 in Justice Parihar's residence.

elaborates by stating that these children are children of a special category of people, where child-friendly concerns may not work. It became clear to me that the judge has a perception of "categories of people", where special needs of children are not seen as a necessary field within the judiciary. Yet again, a socio-economic prejudice prevailed over just decision-making.

Socio-legal Discrimination Against Women

A case in the western city of Jaipur eight years ago where a court ruled "that five upper caste Hindu men were unlikely to have raped a lower caste woman", shows yet another plagued delivery of "justice". The five were cleared of the gang rape of the 43-year-old woman, who was campaigning against the traditional practice of child marriage in Rajasthan. The capital of India, New Delhi, is to set up special courts to deal with cases of rape that will be prosecuted and judged by women. However, the question is, will the delivery of justice be based on justice or social discrimination with a woman judge sitting on the bench? Is the issue about gender inequality or is it about socio-cultural perceptions? The result is yet to be seen.

The social reform movement in India targets several social practices that are against women such as child marriage, *sati* (self-immolation by the widow on the funeral pyre of the husband, a social practice among some Hindu communities), widow remarriage restriction, polygamy, the *purdah* system and female infanticide. In 1929, an all-India

Act banning *sati* was passed. It is truly paradoxical that Roop Kanwar, a young widow, was burnt alive to become a *sati* in 1987 in Deorala, Rajasthan. The tradition of *sati* thrives in parts of north and north-west India where women worship the patron female god of *sati* in temples. The gender discrimination and violence against women have had a profound effect on the sex ratio in India. The child sex ratio (female children per 1,000 male children under five years of age) has been dropping for the past 50 years with the decade of 1991-2001 registering a steep decline from 945 to 927. The existing social relations have reinforced crimes on girl-children and women beginning, in many cases, even before birth in the form of foeticide, infanticide, dowry deaths, and honour killings.[145]

In another unprecedented incident in the Indian city Nagpur in August 2004, a huge mob of women lynched serial rapist and dreaded criminal Akku Yadav and killed him on his way to a local court. When the court arrested four women for the crime, 400 women volunteered to surrender before the court to secure the release of the women who were charged with the criminal's murder. Most media presented the incident as a bizarre legal case rather than focusing on the suffering and anger of the women against the legal-judicial system that gives little justice to women affected by violence such as rape and torture. However, even women's groups are divided on the

145. Kiran Prasad, 'Women's Movement and Media in India: Reshaping Notions of Power,' *Women in Action*, Issue 1 (2002).

emerging power of women to settle scores with criminals using violent means. Some regard this response as a powerful strategy to restructure the insensitive police and legal structures. Others believe that there is the danger of women also being branded criminals if they engage in murder as justice for the crimes suffered by them.[146]

Domestic Violence Against Women and the Law

Violence against women at home is the most pervasive form of human rights abuse. Domestic violence was declared a Human Rights issue for the first time at the United Nations Conference in 1994. Psychologists say domestic violence wreaks havoc on the personality of a woman. The constant threat of violence creates a feeling of helplessness, which destroys a woman's sense of self. The intermittent use of rewards creates yet more confusion in a woman's mind.

One slap a day for a woman is almost a matter of culture in some parts of our country and society, so where and how do we start sensitizing people to violence against women being a crime — in all forms, mental, physical and emotional? The International Centre for Research on Women (ICRW) suggests 80 per cent men from Punjab think violence is justified if the wife is "disrespectful" and 60 per cent justify it if the wife "does not follow instructions". The National Human Rights Commission of India (NHRC) has emphasized the need for opening more than one women's

---

146. Ibid.

police *thanas (*district-based police offices) in every district in different states to deal with crimes against women, but what is being done about the "cultural belief"? Does the law deal with this? Every six hours, a young, married woman is burnt alive, beaten to death or forced to commit suicide, and one in five continues to face domestic violence from the age of 15. This, when violence against women has been recognized as a human rights violation. Victims of violence, physical, sexual and even psychological, these women are today a statistic in the National Family Health Survey (NFHSII). What is more shocking is the fact that social customs and attitudes, which still consider women inferior, abet domestic violence.[147]

Section 498A of the Indian Penal Code (IPC) covers domestic violence. Until the enactment of the recent Protection of Women from Domestic Violence Act, Section 498A was the sole law to protect (married) women from domestic violence. However, Section 498A has been mired in controversy ever since its insertion in the IPC in 1983. Various studies (including a Tata Institute of Social Sciences study of 1999) indicated that the number of cases registered under Section 498A were miniscule compared to the prevalence of domestic violence. Yet allegations of misuse of Section 498A have been voiced consistently by many, including the Malimath Committee on reforms of the Criminal Justice System and Justice J.D. Kapoor of

---

147. Parul Sharma, 'Critical Case: Combating Violence,' *Tehelka the People's Paper*, June 25, 2005.

the Delhi High Court in *Savitri Devi vs Ramesh Chand.* The Bill defines domestic violence as "habitually assaulting or making the life of the aggrieved person miserable by cruelty of conduct, even if such conduct does not amount to physical ill-treatment, or forcing the aggrieved person to lead an immoral life or otherwise injuring or harming the aggrieved person."

The government also initiated a study on the functioning and implementation of Section 498A. The Bureau of Police Research and Development under the Ministry of Home Affairs (MHA) commissioned N.K. Shinghal, a retired police officer, who in a 'statistically' heavy report, referred solely to "views and comments" when referring to "quite substantial" misuse of the provision. This appeared to be sufficient for the government which, in August 2003, based on the Shinghal Report and the Malimath recommendations, introduced the Criminal Law (Amendment) Bill 2003 to amend Section 498A.[148]

In the object and reasons of the Bill, the then Home Minister L.K. Advani stated: "It has been widely reported that this provision has been misused and is also harsh as it is non-compoundable." However, when the Home Ministry was asked for this data on misuse in a question in Parliament in December 2003, the Minister of State for Home Affairs, I.D. Swami, stated, "There is no information

---

148. Bikram Jeet Batra, 'Critical Case: Domestic Violence,' *Tehelka the People's Paper*, October 15, 2005.

available with the government.." There is no doubt that there are cases of misuse of Section 498A, but that is true of any other law.

The minister's reply in Parliament should have ended the debate. However, the constitutionality of Section 498A was challenged in the Supreme Court in *Sushil Kumar Sharma vs Union of India and others.*[149] Not only did the court uphold the constitutionality of Section 498A, it also rebuked Justice J.D. Kapoor, asking him to save his generalized observations and views for seminars or workshops. Unfortunately, the Supreme Court too made generalizations, suggesting that the misuse of Section 498A unleashed a "new legal terrorism".

A recent empirical study by the Delhi-based Centre for Social Research found that no more than 6.5 per cent of cases under Section 498A were found to be false by the investigating agency. This figure is likely to reduce further as the creation of civil remedies under the new domestic violence legislation will allow victims to deflect pressure from police, relatives and lawyers to file criminal charges where unnecessary.[150]

Article 21 of the Indian Constitution regulates the right to life, and Article 14 states equality before law for all citizens. Article 14 prohibits legislative arbitrariness. In *Excel Wear*

149. 2005 6 SCC 281.

150. Bikram Jeet Batra, 'Critical Case: Domestic Violence,' *Tehelka the People's Paper*, October 15, 2005.

vs Union of India, one of the judges underlined that the word "life" in Article 21 of the Constitution does not mean mere animal existence.[151] Furthermore, the right visualized by this article is to live a dignified life.

Yet, in *Harvinder Kaur vs Harmander Singh* 1984, the Delhi High Court abruptly stated: "Introduction of Constitutional Law in the home is most inappropriate. It is like introducing a bull in a china shop. It will prove to be a ruthless destroyer of the marriage institution and all that it stands for. In the privacy of the home and married life neither Article 21 nor Article 14 have any place. In a sensitive sphere which is at once intimate and delicate the introduction of the cold principles of Constitutional Law will have the effect of weakening the marriage bond." Seemingly, the privacy referred to and preferred by the court of law has created a silent victim of domestic violence where constitutional principles stand outside the four walls of violence, now not even bothering to look inside.

Women of the new generation, particularly in the post-reforms era, are facing great challenges where they have to reconcile their "traditional roots" with the "modern values" of a global culture. Surely, economic reforms alone cannot transform the social landscape of India. There must be a parallel attitude change, imbuing of new values and progressive action that must be communicated to each and every citizen at an early age if the coming generation of women are to be empowered.

---

151. AIR 1979 SC 25.

What the law and the law-making authorities forget to address most of the time is the "reason" for certain violence, and why an offender becomes an offender. There surely is some sort of violence going on in the head of the potential or full-fledged offender as well. Here it's a matter of a violation of the real culture surrounding gender equality in our country. These are questions which may amount to viable legislation and more impacting measures. Discussions and efforts such as Mahila Lok Adalats (Women's Fast Track Courts), Family Courts, Crisis Centres, Community Policing Initiatives are somewhat moving, but the issue of cultural beliefs, is standing still. A value-based education system is the key to uplift women according to the NHRC. Education can not only bring about a discernible change in the attitude of women, especially those residing in the rural areas, but can also equip them with a tool to raise their voice against domestic violence, as stated by the NHRC. However, when one side is sensitized, namely the survivor/victim of domestic violence, and the offender sensitization is not even looked at, we may find ourselves having created even a more dangerous situation for the survivor/victim.

13. The Right to Mental Health

Article 12 of the Covenant on Economic, Social and Cultural Rights, provides that states "recognize the right of everyone to the enjoyment of the highest attainable standard of physical and mental health." The General Comment is intended to provide states and the general public with an elaboration of the meaning and implications of the brief Article 12, but with 65 paragraphs and 65 notes, the Comment suffers from being overly comprehensive, and somewhat unclear on what status right to mental health should be given. The General Comment does not explicitly mention mental health. However, it opens up a new era of appreciation of the relationship between health and human rights. It makes clear that the right to health is not to be understood as a right to be healthy. It points out that the right to health "includes certain components which are legally enforceable." The comprehensive right to health as defined in the General Comment is:

> ...an inclusive right extending not only to timely and appropriate health care but also to the underlying determinants of health, such as access to safe and potable water and adequate sanitation, an adequate supply of safe food, nutrition and housing, healthy occupational and environmental conditions, and access to health-related education and information, including on sexual and

> reproductive health. A further important aspect is the participation of the population in all health-related decision-making at the community, national and international levels.

The Indian government spends just 0.83 per cent of its total health budget on the mentally ill, leaving aside victims of crime and their mental health problems completely.[152] Furthermore, mental disorders are severely out of proportionate understanding by the international and national communities. Mental health disorders account for nearly a sixth of all health-related disorders. In spite of this, India has just 0.4 psychiatrists and 0.02 psychologists per 100,000 people, and 0.25 mental health beds per 10,000 people. It is estimated that in 2000, mental disorders accounted for 12.3 per cent of disability adjusted life years and 31 per cent of years lived with disability. Projections suggest that the health burden due to mental disorders will increase to 15 per cent of disability adjusted life by 2020.

Thus, mental disorders account for nearly a sixth of all health-related disability.[153] In the 1970s, Arthur Pearl wrote an article entitled *'The Poverty of Psychology'* in which he commented that "psychologists as a group, along with

152. Atlas: 'Country Profiles on Mental Health Resources 2001', World Health Organization, Geneva.
153. Soumitra Pathare, Less than 1% of our health budget is spent on mental health, www.infochangeindia.org

other social scientists, have been guilty of refusing to accept the challenges that poverty presents to a society of unparalleled affluence.''[154] Harper (1996) claims that psychology as a discipline has not learnt, and argues that one of the reasons that the field had not contributed well to the fight against poverty was because of its over-reliance on attribution theory, which was not adequate to the task.[155]

The trauma that the victims of crime go through because of the crime itself is just the beginning of the journey towards attaining justice. The investigation procedure and the justice administration system are much more traumatizing and victimizing. The victims of crime are not paid much importance because they are not a vote bank and therefore not placed high on the political agenda. The old-fashioned training programme for mental health professionals has resulted in their role becoming that of a technician. There is a lack of conceptual inputs and capacity to think. It is the right of a victim of crime to receive justice. Justice means providing to the victim treatment, rehabilitation and monetary compensation. It is the courts of law which have to provide justice so as to cover al these aspects. Injuries incurred by victims are physical and mental. The courts, when granting justice,

154. D.J. Harper, 'Poverty and Discourse' in S.C. Carr, and T.S. Sloan (eds) *Poverty and Psychology: From Global Perspective to Local Practice*. New York: Kluwer-Plenum (2001).
155. D.J. Harper, 'Accounting for Poverty: From Attribution to Discourse'. *Journal of Community & Applied Social Psychology*, 6 (1996), pp. 249-265.

take into consideration only the physical injuries, which in most cases are not of a very serious nature. However, there are categories of cases where though the physical harm may be capable of healing in a short period of time, the mental agony and trauma does not heal with such speed.

Victims of trauma-related physical and sexual assaults face the greatest risk of developing Post-Traumatic Stress Disorder (PTSD). Women are about twice as likely to develop PTSD as men. These include survivors of domestic or intimate partner violence, rape or sexual assault, physical assault such as mugging or car-jacking and random violent acts such as those that take place in public, in schools or in workplaces.

A victim of crime who is undergoing trauma needs to be treated with care. Immediately after the incident he is asked to repeat the incident again and again. The facilities with regard to emergency reception of victims of crime is lacking to a great extent in our country. There are no psychiatrists to deal with the trauma-stricken victims. Moreover, the victims who do not have signs of serious physical injury are released immediately without any psychiatric treatment. There are also no provisions in the Indian Mental Health Act to admit a person suffering from psychiatric illness and needs detention for treatment in emergency. The courts in cases call upon psychiatrist as expert witnesses. However, the irony is that they are closed questions and are allowed to answer the questions in an explanatory manner. Therefore, the court does not fully utilize the service of psychiatrists.[156]

> *Much of the world is facing rapid economic reforms and social change, including economic transitions that are linked to alarming rates of unemployment, family breakdown, personal insecurity and inequality of income. Poverty remains a reality for much of the world, and mostly affects women. ... Women face great pressures through a range of gender-based disadvantages, and huge numbers experience physical and sexual violence, resulting in high rates of depression and anxiety disorders. Young people, particularly street children and those exposed to violence, are undergoing social upheaval, which is accompanied by climbing suicide rates. In many parts of the world, mental health systems are poorly funded and organized.*

Report of the Ministerial Round Tables: Mental Health, 54th World Health Assembly, May 2001. WHO, Geneva

The new millennium marked several initiatives in the field of mental health. The Government of India has accorded

156. Parts of a paper presented by Dr. Mathiharan, Expert Forensic Medicine Chennai, at the National Convention on Human Rights and Mental Health October 29-30, 2004 Chandigarh; "A Restorative Justice System for Victims of Crime."

high priority to the development of community-based mental health care services during the Tenth Five Year Plan with an allocation of Rs. 190 crores, up from Rs. 28 crores in the Ninth Five Year Plan. Following the Erwardi tragedy in August 2001, the Supreme Court had directed several remedial measures to be taken in the area. A survey of women and children in the prisons of Andhra Pradesh revealed that almost all were "suffering from a disturbed mind in one way or another "and that women face even greater problems when they are released from jail: "the taint of their offences, their alienation from the families and the stigma of the jail sentences stays with them almost forever." What the situation may be for children can only be imagined.

India has a high rate of suicides — 89,000 persons committed suicide in 1995, increasing to 96,000 in 1997 and 104,000 in 1998, a 25 per cent increase over the previous year.[157] Hidden in the data on mental health morbidity are two points of particular importance for India:

- The burden of mental disorders is highest among young adults aged 15-44 years, which is the most economically productive section of the community.

- It is projected that developing countries such as

157. WHO '*Suicide Prevention: Emerging from the Darkness*', regional office for South East Asia , New Delhi.

> India will see the most substantial increases in the burden of mental disorders in the next two decades.

Consequently, mental health policies, legislation, community care facilities, and treatments for people with mental illness are not given the priority they deserve. Barriers to effective treatment of mental illness include lack of recognition of the seriousness of mental illness and lack of understanding about the benefits of services. Policy makers, insurance companies, health and labour policies, and the public at large —all discriminate between physical and mental problems.

India and Mental Health Institutions

The Indian experience with institutionalization has not been civilizing. A report prepared for the National Human Rights Commission (NHRC) in 1999 after an empirical study of mental hospitals in the country condemned the state of mental health institutions. "The findings reveal that there are predominantly two types of hospitals," the report said. "The first types do not deserve to be called 'hospitals' or mental health centres. They are 'dumping grounds' for families to abandon their mentally ill member, for either economic reasons or a lack of understanding and awareness of mental illness. The living conditions in many of these settings are deplorable and violate an individual's right to be treated humanely and live a life of dignity. Despite all advances in treatment, the mentally ill in these hospitals are forced to live a life of incarceration."[158]

"The second type of 'hospitals'," the NHRC report continues, "are those that provide basic living amenities. Their role is predominantly custodial and they provide adequate food and shelter. Medical treatment is used to keep patients manageable and very little effort is made to preserve or enhance their daily living skills. These hospitals are violating the rights of the mentally ill persons to appropriate treatment and rehabilitation and a right to community and family life".[159]The conditions of people with mental illness in institutions is an urgent cause for human rights concern. In Gwalior Mental Hospital, for instance, it was found that persons with mental illness were left in nakedness; the explanation was that they tore their clothes if they were given them. Similarly, at Erwadi in Tamil Nadu, patients who were chained to each other at a home for the mentally ill caught fire and killed 28 people in 2001.[160]

> After the incident, the area Deputy Inspector General, the Superintendent of Police and

---

158. Usha Ramanathan, 'For Better Mental Health,' *Frontline*, Volume 18 - Issue 22, October 27 - November 9, 2001.
159. Bali Mahabal Kamayani, *The First Human Rights Legal Resolutions did not Address Rights of Mental Health Consumers*. Worldwide web: http://www.cehat.org/humanrights/mharticle.pdf.
160. Usha Ramanathan, 'For Better Mental Health,' *Frontline*, Volume 18 - Issue 22, October 27 - November 9, 2001.

> the Collector 'rushed' to the spot 'to assess the situation.' Eyewitnesses told the media that, "had their legs and wrists not been chained, they could have escaped the blaze." These eyewitnesses also reported that most inmates were kept chained 'as per normal practice' and that the alarm raised by some of the inmates (when the fire broke out) was ignored by the hostel owners who mistook it for their 'usual cries'.[161]

The press raised the issue. Chaining of mentally ill patients was also a practice, but was of course outlawed by the reforms introduced by the Supreme Court of India that ensure that the fundamental rights of mentally ill institutionalized patients are not violated and that change the way courts deal with patients who attempt suicide.

While the Mental Health Act may come in useful to take action against errant hospitals, it is equally important for the people in general to move away from the stigma associated with mental illness and be more sensitive to the needs of the mentally ill. In most Indian families mental illness within the family is kept under wraps for fear of jeopardizing the matrimonial prospects of marriageable

---

161. Worldwide web: http://indiatogether.org/health/opinions/jabidi2.htm, article by Javed Abidi who is based in New Delhi, where he heads the National Centre for Promotion of Employment for Disabled People.

young men and women. At a recent seminar organized by the Disability Commissioner's Office and Rotary in Bangalore, a courageous mentally ill young man said, "Every day I get up and need to motivate myself to go to work. Most days I succeed, some days I don't, but I don't give up." His employer spoke after him and vouched for his efforts. According to the Superintendent of a halfway home in Bangalore, "The attitude to mental illness can only change if we accept the illness and the treatment for it just as we would for diabetes or blood pressure." [162]

Civil Society Measures: Commendable But Not Always Correct

Civil society groups and NGOs have recognized the lack of insight and priority amongst policy-makers and the legislators when it comes to mental health concerns, and have therefore taken up the battle, generally in an unguided manner. Help-lines, friendly and non-professional counselling is given to patients in need of professional mental health support. The aforesaid can amount to dreadful outcomes, when, for instance, a victim of domestic violence comes to seek what in her view is guidance within the framework of counselling, but instead receives a cultural orientation on how the role of the Indian woman is to compromise and how with time the violence against the victim may reduce. Similarly, many private initiatives

162. Worldwide web: http://indiatogether.org/2003/mar/hlt-nimhans.htm, article by Melanie P. Kumar is a Bangalore-based freelance journalist; she writes on development issues.

where homeless victims and the socially deprived are kept in homes and shelters, and are run based on the concept of "humanity" and "sewa", however, with no training whatsoever, when it comes to the special needs of victims or patients with psychological disorders.[163] It is difficult though to criticize these groups, which have stepped out to provide what our constitutional welfare state has missed out on or is completely overlooking. Not to forget the immense awareness these groups are creating amongst the masses. Further, this civil society volunteerism can be an excuse for the state to withdraw from its role as a provider of health care.

Dr. Tulsi, a clinical psychologist and psychotherapist, states that a great amount of discrepancy exists between what is written in government gadgets and charter about the term "rehabilitation" and what actually goes on in different rehabilitation centres run by district State Rehabilitation Centres, homes and agencies.[164] In fact, the situation is so pathetic, horrible and disgraceful, according to Dr. Tulsi that those who visit these centres will not be able to come back to their normal level of emotional state for quite some time. On the other hand, the "rehabilitation" word used by government and NGOs are also different from each other. Hence, at grass-root level as well there is a discrepancy in understanding this word. An NGO dealing

163. Sewa, is a religious concept of service to mankind.

164. Dr. Tulsi is the President of Deva International Society for Child Care (DISCC), Varanasi, Uttar Pradesh. The interview took place on June 16, 2005.

with physically and visually handicapped children recently distributed 200 crutches and 300 walking sticks for the blind and considered it as "Rehabilitation of 500 handicapped", whereas distributing a sum of Rs. 125 per handicapped per month by an NGO was called "Economic Rehabilitation".

Dr. Tulsi elaborates that it is not correct at all, that these kinds of approaches are wrongly related to rehabilitation. Rehabilitation or habilitation of a child is a very complex and intricate approach and this involves a child in totality not just hand, feet or mouth. It's a multi-disciplinary approach with various models tried one after another, on an extended period of time and involves a full family. It is just not taking a child from a *dhaba* (roadside restaurants on the highways) where he is working as a child labourer, and putting him into the four walls of a state correctional home where even his basic child rights are not protected, where food for survival is a big problem. Now, putting him in a correctional home situation, he is almost in a jail in the name of "rehabilitation". So, there are so many intricate issues before we come up with a proper definition of child rehabilitation. In a simplest way, it is a matter of "getting the fundamental rights back to the child" by governments or NGOs or civil society groups should be the primary concern in the name of rehabilitation.

Prof. R.S. Chaurasia, General Secretary of Bachpan Bachao Andolan (BBA), defines rehabilitation as a proper care coming from parents, where nutritious food along with education are the primary needs of a rescued child.[165] When I queried the mental health conditions of the children, Prof. Chaurasia responded by explaining that the children are intelligent children, which can be seen when they are sent to school. When I mentioned the impact of trauma on the mental health of children, Prof. Chaurasia explained that mental trauma only remains while the child is bonded, and once the child is rescued the mental trauma and the fear is gone. It was elaborated that once a child is convinced that he is free and the rescue enquiry will not harm him, he also becomes free from trauma.

Upon my question as to whether Prof. Chaurasia had experienced "continuing trauma" with any child, the case of Nageshwar was cited. When Nageshwar was seven years old, a *dalal* (middleman) named Sriram came along with four children, lured him from his village in Bihar to a carpet loom with false promises of good education and a bright future. Nageshwar was brought to a carpet loom situated in a remote area of Allahabad, Uttar Pradesh. For seven years, Nageshwar was forced to work between 4 a.m. to 10 p.m. each day, and his employers would often brutally beat him with a *panja,* a tool used for carpet weaving. Further, no wages were paid and two meagre meals were given to him every day. On November 1, 1995, around midnight, Nageshwar helped his two younger brothers, who worked alongside him, As a result his employer burnt

165. The interaction-cum-interview with Prof.Chaurasia took place in the BBA office in Kalkaji, New Delhi, on July 19, 2005.

him with a red hot iron rod, causing irreparable damage to his body. When the villagers heard of this barbarism, they brought it to the notice of the BBA. On November 4, 1995, a BBA activist rushed to the spot and rescued Nageshwar, and he was brought to the Mukti Ashram.[166] When Nageshwar joined the ashram on November 7, 1995, he was "shell-shocked", unable to express anything. After a month of constant medical treatment by doctors and special care and attention from other children, and the ashram staff, he was able to speak and express himself.

The BBA has a four-fold rehabilitation strategy where restoration of childhood, orientation to education, empowerment and leadership skills, and prevention of child labour are the main areas of intervention. Under restoration of childhood, the BBA constantly stress on the "special physical and psychological care" given to the children.[167] Seeking clarification on the activities conducted in the ashram, Prof. Chaurasia explained, that the staff in all the ashrams run by BBA have specific training to take care of the physical and psychological needs of the child.

166. In 1991, Mukti Ashram was begun in the outskirts of Delhi as the first of a transitory residential centre for the rehabilitation and education of rescued bonded child labourers. Mukti Ashram has, according to BBA, not only physically and mentally rehabilitated individual children who have been rescued by BBA but also given a unique archetype to restoration and empowerment of the most vulnerable and neglected children.

167. Worldwide web: http://www.bbasaccs.org/ourashrams/muktiashram.php3

Trained staff such as Master of Social Work (MSW) and other experienced social workers. Further, there is specific staff for vocational training as well, for instance, in carpenting, screen printing, and motor binding. On my question whether BBA has child psychologists or psychologists as staff members, the response was that this particular staff and their services may be expensive and that they would focus on "one type of work". However, Prof. Chaurasia elaborates, there are many women activists in the ashrams, who by their maternal nature and approach can fulfil the aspects of a psychologist.

Mr. Junned Khan, is a senior project manager at Pratham, a child rights organization focusing on promoting education for all children.[168] Mr. Khan has worked extensively with various child rights organizations such as Prayas, Salaam Balak Trust and Don Bosco. He convincingly explains that reasoning surrounding the child victim diminish, the moment child organisations, non-governmental ones, focus solely on education as a pure measure. Mental health intervention, for instance, are rarely looked into. Many homes and centres for children, run by non-governmental organizations have a conventional "house mother approach", where one lady activist takes upon the role of teacher, parent, psychologist and counsellor. According to Mr. Khan, this approach has nothing to do with limited or lack of resources, but the

168. Meeting with Mr. Junned Khan took place in New Delhi, on July 19, 2005. Worldwide web: http://www.pratham.org/

general lack of understanding for the actual needs of a child, and especially the needs of a child victim.

Mr. Khan elaborates by stating that rescue operations on child labour could have been many more. However, the disinterest and the limited number of lawyers willing to represent these children is one strong reason to why there is a meagre understanding of the issue as such.

Elementary education has seemingly become the dominating measure to rehabilitate children, without actually testing education as a successful means for mental development where a child's physical and emotional integrity has been abused. Furthermore, literature seems to have meagre focus on counselling and child labour. Mental health experts have included various categories of violations and counselling techniques for the same, such as sexual abuse, parental conflicts, and divorce. However, the mental health effects on children rescued from labour is fatally missing. Specific mental health strategies must become a prime concern firstly in legislation, impacting on community interventions.

According to Guy Holmes and Craig Newnes, research that indicates para-professionals and non-mental health professionals (e.g. hairdressers) might be just as good as mental health professionals in terms of helping people who talk to them about their problems has led some psychologists to suggest that we should train or supervise these people. They say that their profession is proficient at creating roles for them where they are the experts and therefore have their professional standing and salaries bolstered. This is the same ideology ('psychologists know best') that has them rushing to become clinical supervisors under the new mental health act. They further state: "Perhaps we need a bit more humility. Social workers have a long history of trying to help oppressed communities. Their training is rooted in anti-oppressive practice. In comparison, psychologists are new to the arena, yet our instincts for colonization coupled with the difficulties social workers currently face in doing their jobs in ways that might help rather than monitor disadvantaged communities mean that there are opportunities for our profession. Yet what skills do we bring? We are highly trained in conducting research. But is there really a need for more research that shows how bad poverty is for people? Does research lead to greater attempts by governments and powerful interest groups and industries to alleviate poverty? One irony of the establishment of the poverty line is that poverty can be reduced by doing nothing except moving the line".[169]

Children, Poverty and Mental Health

"A child's gender, class and caste have a significant influence on her or his well-being"[170]

169. Guy Holmes and Craig Newnes, Shropshire County PCT. 'Thinking about Community Psychology and Poverty.' Published in *Clinical Psychology*, 38 (2004).
170. "*Growing up in Asia report*", Worldwide web: http:// news.bbc.co.uk/go/pr/fr/ /2/hi/south_asia/4174012.stm.

The "Growing up in Asia report" states that in India, 60 per cent of all children were classed as "absolutely poor", with almost half of all children under the age of five being malnourished. It states India also has the highest number of working children in the world. India has the largest number of poor children in Asia, with 80 per cent of its 400 million young severely deprived, according to this 2005 report

The Copenhagen Declaration describes absolute poverty as "a condition characterized by severe deprivation of basic human needs, including food, safe drinking water, sanitation facilities, health, shelter, education and information." The World Bank identifies "extreme poverty" as being people who live on less than $1 a day, and "poverty" as less than $2 a day. On that standard, 21 per cent of the world's population was in extreme poverty, and more than half the world's population were poor in 2001.[171]

Conventional Theories on Poverty.[172] Poverty is studied by many social, scientific and cultural disciplines, and explained traditionally in the following manner:

In economics, conventional discourse focuses on two kinds of poverty: absolute and relative. Absolute poverty refers

171. Worldwide web: www.developmentgoals.org
172. Frances Fox Piven, Richard A. Cloward, *Regulating the Poor: The Functions of Public Welfare*, Vintage Books (1993).

to a set standard which is consistent over time and between countries. Relative poverty views poverty as socially defined and dependent on the social context. Poverty is measured either by indices of consumption or of income. Some countries, like the US measure poverty by identifying a minimum dietary or basket of goods; the US poverty line is based on a multiplier of dietary costs. The main conventional measure used in the OECD and the European Union, however, is based on "economic distance", a level of income set at 50 per cent or 60 per cent of the median household income.

In law, there has been a movement to seek to establish universal "human rights" which aim to eliminate poverty.

In education, poverty affects a student's ability to effectively profit from the learning environments. Especially for younger students coming from poverty, their primary needs as described in Abraham Maslow's hierarchy of needs; the need for a safe and stable home, clothes on their backs, and regular meals clouds a student's ability to learn.[173]

Furthermore, in education circles, there is a term used to characterize the phenomenon of the rich getting richer and the poor getting poorer (as it relates to education but easily transfers to poverty in general) is the Matthew effect. The Matthew effect alludes to a line spoken by "the Master" in Jesus's parable of the talents in the Christian Bible:

---

173. *The Right to be Human: A Biography of Abraham Maslow,* Edward Hoffman, McGraw-Hill (1999).

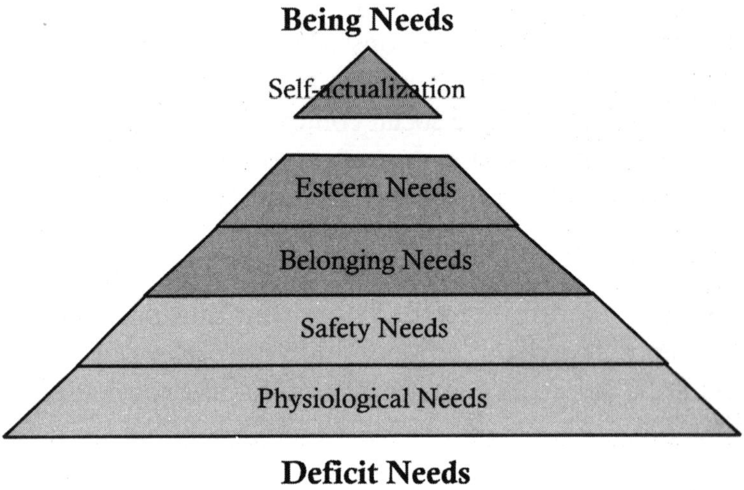

"For unto every one that hath shall be given, and he shall have abundance: but from him that hath not shall be taken away even that which he hath." (Matthew XXV:29, KJV).

This line is sometimes taken in isolation as claiming "the rich get richer and the poor get poorer": taken in context it asserts that ambition and risk-taking will be rewarded, while those who fail to utilize the talents loaned to them will be punished.

In politics, the fight against poverty is usually regarded as a social goal and many governments have, secondarily at least, some dedicated institutions or departments. Active interventions may include housing plans, social pensions, special job opportunities, or requirements.[174]

174. Worldwide web: www.wikipedia.org

Psychology and Poverty. Harper *et al.* (1990) found that the most popular explanations for poverty included the inefficiency of national governments in the South, exploitation by other countries and climate.[175] A factor analysis of the results, reported four factors similar to those of Feagin (1972): 'Blame the Poor'; 'Blame Third World Governments'; 'Blame Nature'; and 'Blame Exploitation' (by other countries and the world economic and banking systems). They reported a significant relationship between the 'Blame the Poor' and 'Blame Third World Governments' factors of the CTWPQ and a 'Pro Just World' factor of the Just World Scale. A reanalysis of the data noted that high Just World believers were significantly less likely to agree that the poverty of the South was due to exploitation by other countries, war or the world economic and banking system.[176]

In the 1970s, Arthur Pearl wrote an article entitled 'The Poverty of Psychology' in which he commented that 'psychologists as a group, along with other social scientists, have been guilty of refusing to accept the challenges that poverty presents to a society of unparalleled affluence'.[177]

---

175. Harper, D.J., Wagstaff, G.F., Newton, J.T. and Harrison, K.R. 'Lay Causal Perceptions of Third World Poverty and the Just World Theory', *Social Behaviour & Personality*, 18, (1990), pp. 235-238.
176. D.J. Harper, and P.R. Manasse, 'The Just World and the Third World: British Explanations for Poverty Abroad', *Journal of Social Psychology*, 132(6) (1992), pp. 783-785.
177. D.J. Harper,'Poverty and Discourse' in S.C. Carr, and T.S. Sloan (eds), *Poverty and Psychology : From Global Perspective to Local Practice.* New York: Kluwer-Plenum (2001).

Harper (1996) claims that psychology as a discipline has not learnt, and argues that one of the reasons that the field had not contributed well to the fight against poverty was because of its over-reliance on the attribution theory, which was not adequate to the task.[178]

Poverty and Child Outcomes. Gelles and Conte (1990) note that a change in the rate of child maltreatment is consistent with the change in character and structure of the family and the economy.[179] Krishnan and Morrison (1995), in testing their human ecology theory, although in a Canadian context, to understand child maltreatment, situated child abuse within a broader social context suggesting, "child abuse is not an individual or isolated family problem but a community problem most often related to the social and economic situation of the locale".[180]

The literature relating poverty to child outcomes reflects three major themes. The first theme relates child development directly to factors intrinsic to families living in poverty. These studies include factors such as nutrition

---

178. D.J. Harper, 'Accounting for Poverty: From Attribution to Discourse.' *Journal of Community & Applied Social Psychology*, 6 (1996), pp.249-265.
179. R.J. Gelles, and J.R. Conte, 'Domestic Violence and Sexual Abuse in the Family.' *Journal of Marriage and the Family*, *52* (1990), pp. 1045-1058.
180. V. Krishnan, and K.B. Morrison, 'An Ecological Model of Child Maltreatment in a Canadian Province.' *Child Abuse and Neglect*, 19(1) (1995), pp. 101-113.

and brain development suggesting poverty, and specifically, poor nutrition, places children at risk for later learning, behavioural and developmental challenges.[181] A second theme suggests that the instability of living arrangements and homelessness due to poverty place children at increased risk.[182] This may reflect the inability of children to receive consistent educational opportunities and parent(s) to develop a social network of support to buffer parental stress. Thirdly, a more encompassing framework within which to view the effects of poverty on children is provided by Avison *et al.* (1994).[183] These authors suggest that the 'pernicious' effects of poverty are such that the financial strain results in the combined effects of caregiver strain, lack of social support, lowered self-esteem and maternal distress resulting in childhood vulnerabilities reflected in both internal and external problems.

Willms (2001) noted from the National Longitudinal Study on Children and Youth (NLSCY) that low socio-economic

---

181. E.M. Tanner, and M. Finn-Stevenson, 'Nutrition and Brain Development: Social Policy Implications.' *American Journal of Orthopsychiatry*, 72(2) (2002), pp. 182-193.
182. E.L. Bassuk, J.C. Buckner, L.F. Weinraub, A. Browen, S.S. Bassuk, R. Dawson, and J. Perloff, 'Homelessness in Female-headed Families: Childhood and Adult Risk and Protective Factors.' *American Journal of Public Health*, 87(2) (1997), pp. 241-248.
183. W.R. Avison, K.N. Speechly, C.T.Thorpe, I.H. Gotlib, N.I. Rae Grant, and J. Turner, (1994). 'Single Parenthood, Poverty, and the Health of Mothers and Children: A Stress Process Analysis.' In M.W. Rosenberg (ed.), *Health and Behaviour 1994:Papers and Proceedings*. Kingston, ON: Queen's University.

status was related to behavioural disorders in 4 to 12 year-olds; poor vocabulary development in preschoolers; and mathematics literacy in primary and intermediate school-age students.

Relieving Poverty for Mental Health

Getting children out of poverty can improve their mental health, but it doesn't appear to fix everything. Behavioural problems, such as conduct disorder, seem to decline with increased incomes, yet moving above the poverty line did not help emotional disorders like anxiety and depression. Jane Costello, a professor of child and adolescent psychiatry at Duke University, examined the mental health of 1,420 children selected from rural areas of western North Carolina over an eight-year period. Four years into the study, a casino built by Cherokee Indians led many tribal families in the area out of poverty. Tribal members were more likely than others in the area to be impoverished. The tribal government distributed profits every Cherokee person over 18, around $6,000 per person by the end of the study.

After four years, the once-impoverished children behaved as well as children who had never been poor. However, depression and anxiety levels did not drop significantly. The children who were never poor remained less depressed and anxious throughout the study.

Relieving poverty helped to improve parental supervision,

according to interviews done with the parents. Costello suggests that most of a child's improvement with behaviour disorders can be attributed to better parenting. Emotional disorders, however, are not as easily resolved.[184]

184. *Psychology Today Magazine*, Publication Date: October 21, 2003, (Document ID: 3051), *Psychology Today Magazine*, Sussex Publisher.

14. India and Sex Education: Denying Real Issues

Legal and Political Beliefs Prevailing in India

The Supreme Court in 2005, stated that sex education in schools cannot be brought under the ambit of fundamental rights by making it a part of the right to education. "We cannot make it (sex education) a fundamental right," a Bench comprising Justice Ruma Pal and Justice A.R. Lakshmanan said while dealing with a Public Interest Litigation, which had suggested making sex education in schools compulsory. The NGO, Nari Raksha Samiti, had submitted that sex education in the school curriculum could play a role in checking the rise in rape cases. Though agreeing with the suggestion, the Bench said it cannot be given the status of a fundamental right on the same footing as the right to education.

A couple of years ago, Ram Chandra Purbey, the former state primary education minister for the northern state of Bihar, made the following observation: "Our society is not an open one. Inclusion of sex education in the syllabus can also have an adverse effect". This statement clearly indicates government attitudes on the issue of sex education, and the misconstrued notion of unpleasant effects of people having sex in every possible corner. Dangerously enough, there is no consensus in India over introducing sex and reproductive health education in the school and college syllabus. On the other hand, the reality is that a large population of about 300 million young people is in the age group 12-24 in India. Studies show their growing preference for pre-marital sex. The government, taking a highly moralistic position on this issue, has refused to recognize the magnitude of the problem. The government stress is more on preaching sexual abstinence and faithfulness to an unwilling population rather than making condoms within easy reach.

A survey of youth in Mumbai done by Sexual and Reproductive Health and Rights of Youth concluded that 64 per cent of youth aged 14 to 19 were no longer virgins; 43 per cent of them have visited prostitutes. In another survey by *The Week* magazine some years ago, of unmarried young Indians, 69 per cent of men admitted to pre-marital sex compared to 38 per cent of women. In the 16-19 group, 45 per cent had pre-marital sex, while 27 per cent were 15 years or under and 28 per cent were 20 years or older. In a 2006 survey of 161 youth aged 18-23 conducted in the Punjab and Haryana regions by the non-governmental organization Sambhavv, 62.8 per cent responded by saying that they used blue films and pornographic data as an alternative to no sex education, 91.8 per cent responded that they have been eve/adam teased. The Sambhavv survey somewhere indicates the bizarre situation where lack of sex education force youth to indulge in violence such as pornography and harassment such as sexual teasing. These studies reveal a continuing denial in government speak about the reality in our society. Ignorance and sex can be a troubling and sometimes deadly mix for young people and those living under suffocating societal demands.

Non-governmental organizations have been trying to produce and distribute their own guidebooks to address what they see missing in the school syllabus on sex education, but their efforts have met with opposition.

WHO on Sex Education

Most important and significant is a 1993 survey conducted by the World Health Organization (WHO) of 35 sex education projects showed that sex education in schools did not encourage young people to have sex at an earlier age or more frequently. Rather importantly, the survey showed that early sex education delays the start of sexual activity, reduces sexual activity among young people and encourages those already sexually active to have safer sex. Furthermore, the WHO published a review of 1,050 scientific articles on sex education programmes. Researchers found "no support for the contention that sex education encourages sexual experimentation or increased activity. If any effect is observed, almost without exception, it is in the direction of postponed initiation of sexual intercourse and/or effective use of contraception." Failure to provide appropriate and timely information "misses the opportunity of reducing the unwanted outcomes of unintended pregnancy and transmission of STDs, and is, therefore, in the disservice of our youth," the report called *Effects of Sex Education on Young People's Sexual Behaviour* says.

HIV and Sex Education

There are only 25 community HIV/AIDS care centres across the country. Horrifyingly, most individuals are tested for HIV without their consent and knowledge. Because of the stigma attached to the disease, not many willingly undergo tests or talk about their trauma. Article 21 of the Indian Constitution imposes an obligation on the State to safeguard the right to life of every person. The government hospitals run by the State and the medical officers employed therein are duty bound to extend medical assistance for preserving human life. Failure on the part of a government hospital to provide timely medical treatment to a person in need of such treatment results in a violation of his right to life guaranteed under Article 21.

With more than 4.5 million people infected by HIV, the virus that causes AIDS, India has become the world's second largest hub of the disease, but some of its states are still in denial. That means that India has the second largest population of HIV sufferers after South Africa. A taboo on talking openly about sex has meant that sex education is not taught in schools, and people, especially women, are reluctant to seek treatment for sexually transmitted diseases. According to Dr. Balaji, the National Council of Education Research and Training (NCERT), has so far been playing it safe because of the explosiveness of the issue of sex education, which cannot be separated from AIDS education. "Too many people think that neither is compatible with their notion of Indian culture."

Anjaiah, his wife and six children were thrown out of their village in Cudappah district of Andhra Pradesh when he was diagnosed as being HIV positive and government hospitals refused to admit him. The family was forced to take shelter under a tree. Anjaiah died a few days later. On being refused admission in a government hospital for being HIV positive, Damayanti had to deliver her baby in the hospital corridor and cut the umbilical cord herself. This did not take place in a remote corner of India but in its capital city, New Delhi. When Narsaiyya tested positive for HIV, he was the last to know. The doctor chose to inform his villagers first, even though medical ethics demand that he inform the patient first.

Article 21 of the Indian Constitution imposes an obligation on the State to safeguard the right to life of every person. The government hospitals run by the State and the medical officers employed therein are duty bound to extend medical assistance for preserving human life. Failure on the part of a government hospital to provide timely medical treatment to a person in need of such treatment results in a violation of his right to life guaranteed under Article 21. The government, taking a highly moralistic position on this issue, has refused to recognize the magnitude of the problem. In early 2003 the then Indian Health Minister Sushma Swaraj told the press that the country's AIDS programme had to focus on sexual abstinence and faith rather than just condoms. The government stress is more on preaching to an unwilling population rather than bringing condoms within easy reach.

The Human Rights Watch (HRW) report from 2004 (Future Forsaken) recognizes that children, especially girls, are extremely vulnerable to societal prejudice. Apart from the millions of children living with HIV/AIDS, many others are either orphaned or forced to withdraw from school to care for their sick parents. According to the report, there are approximately 1.2 million Indian children under the age of 15 who have lost one parent or both parents to AIDS.

The Convention on the Rights of the Child, in Article 24 recognizes the right of children to enjoy "the highest attainable standard of health and to facilities for the treatment of illness and rehabilitation of health." Punima J. is seven-years-old, her parents died of AIDS. Her grandfather described her parents' deaths: "The father died first, then the mother committed suicide a few months later, she was positive. She poisoned her daughter at the same time, but we got her treatment and she survived." Punima, who was also HIV-positive, "is continuously sick," her grandfather said, and was "getting medicine [a general antibiotic] from Tamburan and local doctors, but she doesn't regularly take the medicine. She doesn't like it." Punima agreed, "I don't like to take medicine." Similarly, the father of thirteen-year-old Dinesh T. and his fifteen-year-old sister had died of AIDS a year before HRW met Dinesh. Their mother, who was also HIV-positive and increasingly sick, had committed suicide some five months before. The children found the body of their mother, hanging in their home.

The refusal to treat and perform surgical operations, denial of admission in hospitals, marking HIV positive on the beds occupied, refusal to touch objects used by positive patients, wrapping of dead bodies of positive patients in plastic, imposing additional charges for basic services are some of the common discriminatory practices faced.

The added stigma and trauma imposed on HIV/AIDS infected people, and on a child's life is a price our highly moralistic political leaders will pay, when they find themselves preaching Victorian principles, old-fashioned perceptions on sexuality and diseases to a vanished generation.[185]

Sexual Minorities and Sex Education

The questions within persons who experience homosexuality as their reality causes them additional trauma when suffocating demands are placed even on heterosexual behaviour in the society. Though debate about the cause of homosexuality continues, scientists and social theorists tend to agree that nobody chooses to be homosexual. Available data from the US, Canada, Australia, and elsewhere in Europe tend to place the homosexual population between 3-8 per cent of the total population. The question is no longer whether homosexuality is natural, but whether homosexuals should enjoy the same rights and privileges as other citizens. One

---

185. Parul Sharma, 'Critical Case; Aids and Law,' *Tehelka the People's Paper*, August 13, 2005.

of the rights inclusive in the privileges is "the right to be informed". Proponents of comprehensive sex education believe that a common approach to sex education is necessary to reduce risky behaviour such as unprotected sex, and equip individuals to make informed decisions about their personal sexual activity. Additionally, they contend that education about homosexuality encourages tolerance, but does not "turn masses gay" as some conservatives believe.

The silence and shame around the issue of homosexuality is so great and the fear of being isolated and discriminated is so prevalent that a lot of those who are caught by the police prefer to pay the police rather than fight back referring to their Human Rights. Almost none of the cases go to court with the person being let off after he has paid the police officer. Human Rights abuses are actually legitimized by laws which treat homosexuals as secretive, criminal, and so on; the lack of support for them from the educational and legal systems compounds the social misery. Governmental attitudes to homosexuality are worrisomely in line with positions on sexuality, AIDS and sex education itself, the views are not particularly surprising. Naz Foundation, an NGO, had brought an action in the Delhi High Court challenging the constitutionality of Section 377 Indian Penal Code (IPC), which talks of homosexual intercourse as unnatural sex. The Central Government dithered for two years before it filed its response. It did so only after immense pressure from civil society organizations and the passing of several strictures by the court. While its dithering is understandable as a tactic to lose another problematic litigation in the jungle of half a million or so cases clogging the Indian judiciary, the substance of its reply brings to light the culture straitjacket. In paragraph 32 of the reply the government states: "In fact, the purpose of this Section 377 IPC is to provide a healthy environment in the society by criminalizing unnatural sexual activities against the order of nature." And then goes on to add in Paragraph 33: "If this provision is taken out of the statute book, a public display of such affection would, at the most, attract charges of indecent exposure which carry a lesser jail sentence than the existing imprisonment for life or imprisonment of 10 years and fine. While the government cannot police morality, in a civil society criminal law has to express and reflect public morality and concerns about harm to the society at large. If this is not observed, whatever little respect of law is left would disappear, as law would have lost its legitimacy." In other words, seemingly the government maintains that if 'unnatural' sex is not prohibited, the normal social order would break down. Moreover, the issues relating to sexual minorities is not an Indian issue, but more of something which happens in the West.

Women and Sex Education

A school for brides in the central Indian state of Madhya Pradesh teaches women how to be ideal wives by serving their husband and his family, but keeps sex off the curriculum. The 18-year-old Manju Sanskar Kendra funded by businessmen in the state capital, Bhopal, aims to "smooth" a bride's path with a special three-month training course, which includes cooking, sewing and daily prayers. The school charges no fees and boasts of having trained over 4,000 girls between the ages of 18 to 21. However, the bridal finishing school manages to avoid one of the key issues in any marriage, and does not give any sex education or talk about safe sex. "At the school we've been told to please our husbands at all times and have children, which I suppose means sex," explains a 22-year-old "student". Furthermore, and maybe due to the privileged status of men in our country, only 5 per cent of Indian men use condoms according to Dr. Avni Amni at the Centre for Health and Gender Equity. Most parents in India are not aware of their role in imparting sex education, explains Amit Jain, a well-known sex counsellor; "Sex education doesn't even figure at all in the priorities of the Indian parents."

Sex education is also a means to respect a partner, a wife, a husband, a boyfriend, a girlfriend, and a means to respect sexual preferences. It is also a means to question and understand the existence of assault and sexual violence in our country and to increase gender equality. The lack of understanding about sexual issues is more risky, and more likely to lead young people to have unwanted pregnancies, abortions and STDs, and sometimes sex-related violence. There are so many crucial issues at hand, which could be saved and cured by means of sex education.

Child Abuse, Sexual Exploitation and Sex Education

The Delhi-based Sakshi Violation Intervention Centre in a 1997 study that interviewed 350 school children, found that 63 per cent of the girl respondents had been sexually abused by a family member; 25 per cent raped, and over 30 per cent sexually abused by the father, grandfather or a male friend of the family. A 1999 study by the Mumbai-based Tata Institute of Social Sciences revealed that 58 of the 150 girls interviewed had been raped before they were 10 years old. Rahi, a Delhi-based organization that provides support to victims of sexual abuse, reports that of the 1,000 upper and higher-middle class college students interviewed, 76 per cent had been abused as children, 31 per cent by someone known to the family and 40 per cent by a family member, and 50 per cent of them before the age of 12.

Children around the world are sexually abused and exploited in ways that can cause permanent physical and psychological harm. In some cases, police demand sexual services from street children, threatening them with arrest if they do not comply. In detention and correctional facilities children may be sexually abused by staff or are not protected from sexual abuse by other inmates. In refugee camps many children are exploited by adults or sometimes forced to sell their bodies for food. Children working as domestics may be assaulted or raped by employers. Articles 34 and 35 of the Convention on the Rights of the Child forbid sexual exploitation or trafficking of children, and the Committee on the Rights of the Child has devoted time and efforts to the issue, urging governments to crack down on the practice. Other international instruments in human rights, humanitarian law, refugee law, and labour standards protect children against sexual exploitation. In addition, a UN special rapporteur on the sale of children, child prostitution and child pornography investigates these issues. According to UNICEF reports from 2001, children and women subjected to commercial sexual exploitation:

100,000 in the Philippines
400,000 in India
100,000 in Taiwan
200,000 in Thailand
244,000-325,000 in the United States
100,000 in Brazil
35,000 in West Africa
175,000 in Eastern and Central Europe

Another UN report indicates that 125 children per hour are sexually exploited in the world. Internet-related child exploitation is relatively new but it has been the force behind the resurgence of child pornography. The major problem is enforcing the law. Given the millions of web sites, and the ability of paedophiles to encrypt photographs or put them in a code that can only be translated with special software, most police departments are ill-equipped to find such pornography. Moreover, most legal systems in the world do not allow hacking for investigation purposes. The lack of monitoring found in many locations on the Internet enables paedophiles, often using an online persona of a child, a medium to entice. Paedophiles befriend lonely children through contacting them on an electronic bulletin board, asking to be their pen pal, exchanging private messages, and finding out about the child's relationship with his or her parents and friends. Through this communication, the paedophile determines the child's likes and dislikes and uses this information to lure the child. The paedophile then breaks down the child's inhibitions, often by showing him or her photographs of other children engaged in sexual activity, showering the child with love and affection, and convincing the child that he or she is not loved at home. This is called the grooming phase.

The *Report on Laws and Legal Procedures Concerning the Commercial Sexual Exploitation of Children in India* presented by ECPAT International in November 2004, reported that a major obstacle in protecting children in India stems from piecemeal laws that police and law officers find difficult to implement because of inadequate or inconsistent procedures to support implementation, according to the report. A key concern is that child victims of commercial sexual exploitation receive poor legal assistance, if any at all. No special provisions ensure they have access to their own legal counsel so that they are fully informed about legal proceedings and their rights, including their rights as witnesses. The report recommends that India's child protection laws be clarified so that violations are well defined and clear guidance is offered on procedures to implement the law. Police and legal officers would then be better able to enforce child-protection measures, including guaranteeing that children involved in legal proceedings benefit from formalized child-friendly legal procedures and receive legal assistance and appropriate social services.

The actual sexual abuse may be cured or healed through a rehabilitation process, provided the country has recognized rehabilitation as part of its justice system, which is not the case in, for instance, most developing countries. Whatever the attitude towards rehabilitation may be in a country, the awareness with the child that the abuse is documented and easily accessible on the net is a trauma for a lifetime. Besides the untold emotional and psychological damage sexual exploitation causes children, their exposure to HIV is such, that one-third of all prostitutes in Asia are reported to be HIV positive.

The principle of "Hear no evil, See no evil, Speak no evil", has become merely a principle of denial, when child abuse is taking place every day and every moment just a google search away. Strange how we have learnt to live with it when we know that sexual exploitation of children is a social disease that denies children their most basic rights and their human integrity.

However, despite the gravity of the problem, the various facets of child sexual abuse are never discussed within the educational system. Dr. Preethi Menon, a Chennai-based paediatric psychiatrist dealing with child sexual abuse, underlines that "this secrecy has to be broken"; for this, she lays stress on talking to children about sexual abuse, listening to them, believing them, and recognizing symptoms such as physical complaints and behavioural and psychological changes. She says: "Silence does not mean all is fine with the child." Bizarrely, the educational system has missed out on informing its children that the moment an abuse has taken place — something wrong has taken place. This is nothing foreign; most civilized nations use the educational system as a crucial means to inform its children about what amounts to a sexual assault or crime against a minor, and about the various victim support systems. Maybe, it is immature to believe that sensitive issues such as incest would be dealt with in a set-up, which does not even believe in sex education in schools. There is a lack of a system of awareness, where the adult's accountability towards a child fails in the gravest manner.

To a query held now in 2005 on whether starting sex-education at 14 years is too late, about 92.46 per cent respondents have said 'yes' in an 8888 poll. Therefore, the implications are clear the subject must indeed be introduced in schools at the pre-teen level itself.

The US-based non-profit group, Programme for Appropriate Technology in Health (PATH), has projects that target not only students but high school-based sex educators around the world, as, for instance, in Thailand. "It is like being full after eating rice. Once you find out all about it, you don't need to go and try it out or find out about it from somewhere else," a PATH student says. ''In fact, it (sex education) makes you think that it should not be easy to decide to have sex because there are plenty of hassles that can result.'' In short, some youngsters say, they need correct information delivered effectively. ''The more it (sex) is concealed, the more we (teenagers) want to know.''

The World AIDS Day is another reminder to go beyond campaigns to "safe sex and right to sex education". Students must feel comfortable in seeking counselling on sex-related issues. The tactic is to speak the same language as students do and to keep an open mind. There is no right or wrong answer when talking about sex, and every question needs to be answered, no matter how private. This up-front approach would surely decrease the frustrations and aggressions linked to sexuality amongst youth.

15. Conclusion

Mental health concerns must not be seen as an isolated reality of those who have been victims of crime or poverty, or for those who are suffering from some mental illness. This concerns us all, as plural beings, where every person is a host of identities. To be informed about matters on sex and sexuality must be viewed as a matter of upholding mental health concerns. The right to information is not merely a legal provision stating that I have a right to know. No, right to information must initially be seen as directly linked to my right to grow and develop into a balanced and healthy human being.

Furthermore, if the right to life is a part of a constitutional text, also known as a social contract, it is impossible to ignore aspects surrounding a social being. The term *social* is derived from the Latin word *socius*, which as a noun means "an associate, ally, companion, business partner or comrade" and in the adjectival form *socialis* refers to "a bond between people" (such as marriage) or to their collective or connected existence. This companionship, connectedness or bond between peoples must not be based on dreamy notions, where poverty, crime and disparity don't exist. Rather it must coexist with all the aspects concerning the pluralism of human life, taking into consideration that a whole being has rights. The pluralism of human existence is precisely the same as the cycle of human rights, where all rights are inextricably linked; my physical rights with my psychological rights. The aforesaid must be included in each process of justice, i.e. in law-making as well as in the execution of law. This has apparently not been easy to consider, and it has to start by creating a society where the notion of *empathy* rules, inside and outside the court of law.

***

Index